FIFTY DANGEROUS THINGS
(you should let your children do)

Probably The Most Dangerous Pledge You Ever Make

I, _____ will
demonstrate that danger
can be conquered with
skill and determination.
As proof of this, I will complete
the challenges put forth in
this book. Maybe not today,
maybe not this week,
and maybe not this year,
but one day I will check off
every one of these
Fifty Dangerous Things.

Dated, this _____ day
of the _____ month,
in the year _____.

FIFTY DANGEROUS THINGS
(you should let your children do)

By Gever Tulley with Julie Spiegler

For information, write Tinkering Unlimited, P.O. Box 370721, Montara, CA 94037-0721 or send email to publisher@tinkering-unlimited.com.

ISBN-13: 978-0-9842961-0-1
ISBN-10: 0-9842961-0-7

Library of Congress Control Number: 2009941652

www.tinkering-unlimited.com
www.fiftydangerousthings.com

Attention: Schools and Educators
We'd appreciate it if you would refrain from photocopying the entire book, but feel free to copy what you need. Special pricing can be arranged, please contact us for details.

Acknowledgements
We sincerely appreciate all the help we received in creating this book. These are just a few of the many people who have supported this project:

Jennifer Spiegler and Mori Jake Nishihira
Jessica Grunwald Braun
Matt Spiegler
Geetha Reddy
Michael Gough
Mayumi Honda
Steve Davee
Robyn Orr

Special thanks to Liz Smith and her boys Hooper Smith and Josh Michalski and also Katherine and her boys Connor and Brendan.

And all of our wonderful Tinkering School alumni (and their parents and siblings) who assisted with testing: Piper, Fiona, Nik, Gus, Sam, Isaac, Leo, Kate, Charlotte - and many others who inspire Gever every day.

Dedication
This book is dedicated to our bold, caring parents who gave us the opportunity to meet the world on our own terms, then patched us up and sent us off again when we needed it; and to all the parents out there like them.

Disclaimer

This book is for entertainment, enlightenment, and education. We have done our best to be as accurate and clear as possible, but we assume no responsibility for errors or omissions in the content of this book. Nor do we assume liability for any damages resulting from actions taken as a result of any information included this book.

Keep in mind, results may vary. Remember that that's half the fun: figuring out your own, unique solution to every project or challenge. We disclaim any liability for injury that may result from any use - proper or other-wise - of the information in this book. We do not guarantee that any of the information is complete, safe, or accurate. Don't forget that we did entitle the book "Fifty Dangerous Things"! Please exercise good judgment and common sense.

Remember to obey all laws and respect all rights - including property rights and individual rights.

And above all - have fun!

Contents

Contents

Foreword

One might argue that there are a lot of dangerous things in this book for children, and anyone else, to do. I argue that NOT doing these things is ultimately a more dangerous proposition for ourselves, and society. These activities offer real ways to encounter phenomena first-hand, and provide opportunities to make careful observations, and generate new questions. Experiments with chemical and mechanical systems can lead to meaningful practice with tool-use and construction methods. And getting "stuck" can be scary, silly, and fun. Engagement with the world in these ways usually occurs in Kindergarten classrooms, or graduate level programs at universities. They are often the most powerful in terms of cognitive development, but unfortunately, this type of behavior is seldom endorsed in our schools, street corners, or homes.

This book does that. It is a guide to developing better questioners, tinkerers, experimenters, and thinkers. These are the tools with which children ultimately become inquisitive members of society and are the underpinnings of our next generation of inventors, innovators, and leaders. So I encourage everyone, young and old, experienced or not, to try everything in this book. You may begin seeing the familiar in an unfamiliar way, to question what you're told before making a decision about something, and develop the capacity to first "try it" before deciding that you "don't know how to do it." Go ahead, get started; the first dangerous thing is the hardest.

Mike Petrich
Learning Studio Director
Exploratorium
2009

Introduction
For Kids

Hello! My name is Gever and I started Tinkering School. Our school is different; we don't have classes, we just do one thing all day long: we build stuff! Kids get to use real materials and real tools, but they have to show that they are responsible enough to do it.

We only have one rule at Tinkering School, and, before you read any further, you have to promise to obey it. Ready? The rule is:

Don't Hurt Yourself Or Anyone Else.

That's the only rule. Oh, you may get a few little cuts and scrapes, maybe a bruise - that's inevitable. But don't hurt yourself just because you didn't pay attention to what you were doing.

It might seem impossible that your parents were once kids who ran around and maybe even climbed trees, but believe me when I tell you that it's true. And, just like kids, every parent is different. What one parent feels comfortable letting their kids do, may be almost impossible for another parent to consider letting their kids do.

It's the same with kids: what is safe for one kid might be crazy for another kid. Would you go out and try a triple flip on the flying trapeze just because you saw a kid do it at the circus? No, you'd practice first, learn how to do a single flip and work your way up to the triple (at least I hope you would).

The activities in this book can all be done safely, but that doesn't mean that they are all safe for you. You might need to get better at making fires before you should try to melt glass, and you might need to walk home from school for a while to show that you can be trusted to ride public transit across town.

Many of the activities take some time, some planning, and, some-times, a grown-up. As with all potentially dangerous endeavors, you have to talk to a grown-up about each project before you do it. If the two of you decide that the activity is not right for you now, use the notes page to write down when you think you will be able to do it. You might write "Do this when I'm 10" or "Do this after I learn how to make a good fire."

I wrote this book because I believe that the best way to be safe is to learn how to judge danger. By doing these kinds of activi-ties and projects, you will develop a good sense of the difference between things that are dangerous and things that you just need to be careful with.

Be safe, and have fun.

Key
Guide to Page Contents

|'|'|'|'|'|'|'|'|'|'|'|'|'|
DURATION

This meter tells you the amount of time you can expect to spend on the given topic. The meter goes from 0 to 8 hours. This meter is showing that the project will take between 2 and 3 hours. Your actual time may vary.

|'|'|'|▲|'|'|'|'|'|
DIFFICULTY

This meter gives you a sense of how hard or complicated a topic will be. The meter goes from "easy" to "very difficult," and is currently showing "pretty easy." This is only a general guideline, and what may be easy for one person may be hard or impossible for someone else.

GET DIRTY

Hazard symbols are used to warn you of some possible dangers you may encounter. The instructions will help you avoid those dangers, but it is up to you to be vigilant, careful, and responsible.

```
Supplementary Data
```

Every topic includes some interesting facts and details. There may be clues in the Supplementary Data section that will help you do the project, or it may just be fun information to think about.

ACTIVITY	**EXPERIENCE**
SKILL	**PROJECT**

The color on the page tells you what kind of topic it is.

For the majority of projects in this book, you will need some supplies and materials other than just yourself. These are useful items that you will want to have on-hand for virtually all your projects:

☐ Scratch Paper - you always need a bit of paper for something
☐ Pen or Pencil - for taking notes and making marks when measuring things
☐ Scissors - to cut paper, plastic, and cloth as necessary
☐ Paper Towels or Rags - for quick clean up of accidental spills
☐ Old Tablecloth or Newspapers - to protect your work surface
☐ Safety Goggles - sunglasses can work, but you want to be sure you have complete coverage and can see clearly; it's a small investment to protect your eyes!
☐ Tape - duct tape is most useful, but transparent or masking tape will work too (and is best for some projects)

When doing any of these projects, be sure you pick an appropriate place to work: grown-ups do not always appreciate having science experiments done on the new dining room table. If you cover it properly, almost any surface can be protected, but the best one is a workbench or project table specifically designated for project work.

Over time you will collect tools and materials that you like to use. Consider getting a toolbox or carton that you can keep everything organized in.

The duration indicators are guidelines. Some activities might take much longer, or you may decide you want to spend a lot more time on a project than what is shown. You might even have to make a plan to do some projects during vacation or on a school holiday.

Difficulty indicators are also guidelines. You might find some projects much easier than suggested, but an unfamiliar skill might turn out to be much harder than estimated. There is no "right" answer - the guidelines are provided only to assist in selecting which Dangerous Thing you want to try next.

Every one of the Fifty Dangerous Things has its own web page, which is listed in each Progress box. On it you can share ideas, upload photos of your projects, or just see what other kids have done. http://www.fiftydangerousthings.com

Introduction
For Grown-ups

My name is Gever Tulley, and in 2005 I started an experiment called Tinkering School. It's a place where children are given an opportunity to build big things using real tools and materials. This ongoing endeavor has taught me a lot about what children can accomplish, and how responsible they can be, when given the chance. The projects in this book bring a bit of the Tinkering School experience into your home. This book is an invitation to explore the world with the children in your life.

Imagine a world where we have finally rounded every corner, hidden all the knives, and put safety rails around every gully and tree, where all the floors are non-skid, and pointy scissors are only given to those with drivers licenses. Is it a safer world? Will our children finally be absolutely and perfectly protected? Can we finally let them back out to play and frolic like we did when we were young? Will their young minds be filled with ideas and wild dreams as they climb on the hypoallergenic play structures? Will their imaginations spin whole fantasies out of plastic toys the way we did when we held a long crooked stick in our hands, looked down the length of it, and felt our hearts stir? Can we let them out of our sight, secure in the knowledge that the GPS tracking unit built into their cell phone will get them safely back home?

Of course we must protect children from danger - that's the promise we make to them as a society. But when that protection becomes over-protection, we fail as a society because children don't learn how to judge risk for themselves. So we must help them understand the difference between that which is unknown (or unfamiliar) and that which is truly dangerous.

Here's a thought-provoking question: at what age would you feel comfortable giving your child a sharp stick to play with? Now, take a moment to consider the risks and start from age two and go up until you are sure you could just hand them the sharp stick and not feel compelled to say "be careful...."

Did the phrase "poke out an eye," or something like it, leap to mind? It's OK, we're programmed to think of things like that as soon as we say "sharp stick." Now consider this: some of the Inuit peoples give their toddlers knives. Imagine a three-year-old sitting on the floor using a sharp knife - the mind fairly boggles. Having considered that, rest assured that the Inuit love their children as much as we do; it's just that seal blubber makes up a significant portion of their diets and blubber is notoriously hard to bite through. So the parents give the children razor-sharp knives and teach them how to hold the blubber in their teeth, pull it with one hand and cut it with the other. During this operation, the tip of the knife will pass within millimeters of the tip of the child's nose.

Suppose that we added a knife-skills program to kindergarten - what kind of knife would the school-board approve? I feel certain that it would be no more dangerous than a plastic spork, and about as useful.

We all pretty much agree that reading, writing, and math are considered necessary for survival these days. We have specially-designed books and television programs that help toddlers acquire the precursor skills that are the building blocks for learning to read, write, and count. We have elaborate games that go to great lengths to mask their goal of teaching these precursor skills. The game context makes the rote learning more palatable to children, or so the packaging would have the parent or grandparent believe. But we don't have many games, or books, or TV shows that help children become competent.

Let me assure you, in case you are starting to wonder, that I believe reading, writing and math skills are important skills that children should acquire. These are the gateways to the acquisition of almost all other knowledge and, I dare say, competence. But the child who grows up in the woods will always be more comfortable there than the child who reads about wood lore in a book, just as the child who actually squashes a penny on a railroad track will have a deeper, more concrete understanding of the physics involved than the one who watches a video of it.

What is competence? I measure competence by the manner in which we approach a difficult problem in the real world. A competent person will examine the context of the problem, look at the tools and raw materials, and begin postulating possible solutions, performing small experiments that test the critical aspects of their postulate and start forming a working solution. Competent people overcome setbacks and treat failures as feedback, which they incorporate in the ongoing, evolving solution to the problem. The competence-challenged person will give up when the problem has no easy or obvious solution, or will abandon their solution the first time it fails.

Competent people tend to poke at things to see how they work. They ask questions and when they don't get answers, they try to figure things out. They see problems as puzzles instead of obstacles. They tend to know a little about a lot of different topics. We often recognize competence in people who are self-confident. Competence is a component of self-confidence, as it gives us the confidence that, in any given situation, we will be able handle whatever happens.

How do we build competence in children? We do it by giving children opportunities to distinguish that which is truly dangerous from that which merely contains an element of risk; we introduce them to risk through measured, supervised exposure; we teach them how to explore safely, and set them on a path to exploring on their own.

So, despite appearances, this book is really about safety. Each of these activities contains an element of risk: use them as an opportunity to discuss those risks with your child. We mitigate risk with "scaffolding" - planning, practicing by steps, and taking reasonable precautions. Let children practice climbing trees, and they will learn to do it safely. If you never let them climb a tree, they will eventually do it anyway, possibly in the most unsafe manner possible. Or they may never do it at all, which might be the greater tragedy.

These are not recipes to be followed absolutely; these are general guidelines that assume there is necessarily going to be some improvisation. In real life you never have exactly the right bit of rope, or the perfect tool, when a problem arises - this is how we learn how to solve problems with the materials at hand, to make things work despite having lost some of the parts, to persist in spite of the odds. That is the true nature of tinkering.

On Age
Every child is unique; your child may be exceptional in one manner but awkward in another. There are a lot of activities in here - it is up to you and your child to decide which ones are best to do now, and which they will have to wait to do when they are older or more experienced. If you can't let them do something now, consider writing your requirements on the notes page opposite each topic. That way they can check your requirements instead of constantly asking if they are old enough, tall enough, or responsible enough to do it.

On Why
You might ask why you should let your child glue their fingers together. In the back of the book you will find a section called "Why?" For each topic, we supply at least one reason why you might consider letting them undertake the activity. Some reasons are pragmatic (knowing how to make a fire is a useful skill), and some are more aesthetic (sleeping under the stars is just a great thing to do). You may have better reasons and/or you may disagree with our reasons, but at the very least, it can be the basis of an interesting discussion with your child.

On Tinkering
If you are raising a young tinkerer, know that there are activities in this book that will require your guidance and, sometimes, your assistance.

When it comes time to help, resist the urge to tell them how to do it (unless there is imminent danger, of course). Instead, try acting like a robot that only does what you are told. Be the big, strong or dexterous hands that they need, and, most importantly, let them fail. Then help them figure out why they failed and how to work around it - even if it means starting over.

You are a super hero; you are endowed with the power of supervision. Use it wisely, and judiciously, and not only will your child surprise you, you may surprise yourself.

FIFTY DANGEROUS THINGS

SHOCK

☐ 9-volt Battery

DURATION **DIFFICULTY**

WARNING

Do not hold the battery to your tongue for more than a few seconds at a time.

```
Supplementary Data

Normally, the nerves in your tongue
are activated by tiny chemical recep-
tors in your taste buds. The surface
of your tongue is divided into dif-
ferent specialized regions that are
tuned to notice specific flavors. The
battery has no specific flavor of its
own, but the electrical current that
runs between the terminals activates
a random collection of nerves on your
tongue causing you to experience a
sensation of exaggerated, but non-
specific, taste.

The tongue may be one of the earli-
est sense organs to evolve. You can
imagine how important it might be, to
an early multi-celled creature float-
ing around in the primordial soup,
to be able to taste things before
eating them. In humans, the tongue is
wired directly to the brain through
little holes in the skull, bypassing
the spinal cord completely.

Early batteries may have been made in
clay pots with copper and lead plates.
Evidence of these were found in the
ruins of a 2000 year old village near
modern Baghdad. Archeologists suggest
that lemon juice could have been used
as the electrolyte, and recent recon-
structions confirm that it would have
generated electricity.
```

HOW-TO

You are about to give yourself a tiny shock. It won't exactly hurt, but it will feel strange.

1. Hold the battery in your hand, with the terminals facing up.

2. Stick out your tongue.

3. Take a deep breath.

4. Think about kangaroos hopping around in a field of flowers. This is really just to heighten the anticipation - you can think about anything you want.

5. Quickly touch the metal terminals of the battery to your tongue.

6. Try again, but hold it there for a full second.

How would you describe the sensation to someone who has never done it? Does it have a taste or is it something else?

If you would like to experience something similar, chew on a wad of aluminum foil for a few seconds (be sure not to swallow any!). The foil will create a weak electric current when it contacts the acid in your saliva. If you have any fillings, you may experience an odd tingling in your teeth as the metal in the fillings conducts the electricity to the nerves nearby.

02 | Play in a Hailstorm
Get up close and personal with Mother Nature

PROJECTILES

COLD

BUMPS AND BRUISES

REQUIRES

☐ Hailstorm
☐ Mixing Bowl
☐ Rain Gear
☐ Gloves or Oven Mitts

DURATION   **DIFFICULTY**

WARNING

Hail comes in many sizes, ranging from tiny pebbles to as big as a grapefruit. Do not go outside if the individual hail pellets are much larger than a pea.

Lightning can occur whenever there is hail. If you hear any thunder, or the local weather forecast is predicting lightning, then do not go outside with a metal bowl on your head.

HOW-TO

1. Choose your bowl. A big metal mixing bowl is ideal; plastic bowls don't make as much noise but will also work. A cookie sheet can be used, but is hard to keep over your head without holding it tight with both hands, especially if it's windy.

2. Suit up. Wear a rain coat, gloves or oven mitts, and sturdy pants that will protect you from being stung by the hail. Hold the bowl over your head.

3. Enter the hailstorm. If it's not too windy, try to balance the upside down bowl on your head without holding it, so that you can really hear the hail hitting it.

You could use an umbrella, but would it be as silly or as fun? Sometimes the point of doing something is not to find the "best" way to do it, but to discover the most fun way.

Turn the bowl right-side up and you may notice that the hail has a tendency to bounce out. If you would like to catch hail, a towel or a pillowcase may be more effective than a bowl.

Supplementary Data

Hail pellets are formed when strong updrafts inside large clouds lift rain up to altitudes where it freezes. The process can repeat multiple times: each trip from the bottom to the top of the cloud adds a new layer of frozen water to the pellet. A large pellet will reveal an onion-like structure if you cut it in half, one layer for each trip through the cloud.

Pellets can stick together in the cloud to form irregular lumps of even greater size, in a process called "wet growth." The largest hail stone ever recorded was 7 inches in diameter and the heaviest weighed more than one and half pounds.

Meteorologists preserve hail for further study by packing it in dry ice. However, due to the effects of sublimation when water is kept below freezing, the hail still eventually decays.

PROGRESS

Date: ___ / ___ / ___   I did it! ☐

www.fiftydangerousthings.com/topic/02

CLONKED

BUMPS AND BRUISES

REQUIRES

☐ Lawn or Soft Play Area

DURATION   **DIFFICULTY**

WARNING

Whenever you are learning a new skill - especially one that involves flinging yourself at the ground - it's important to start slowly and think through each move before you do it. Note that we're talking about a forward roll, not a flip.

Supplementary Data

Somersaults and cartwheels have been banned at some schools because of the potential for injury - a perfect example of what is referred to as "fear-based" decision making. The possibility that a child might be injured by doing a somersault is too scary to think about, so the activity is banned instead of teaching students how to do it safely.

A somersault is a forward roll in which your back contacts the ground. A cartwheel is when just your hands touch the ground, and a flip is when nothing touches the ground except your feet.

The world record for somersaulting was set by Ashrita Furman when he covered more than 12 miles as he performed 8341 consecutive somersaults without stopping.

HOW-TO

At first, somersaulting may not seem very useful. But, if you practice it until it becomes second nature, you may find yourself somersaulting instead of scraping up your hands or knees next time you trip and fall.

1. Prepare. Find a nice clear area that is free of sticks and rocks.

2. Stand with one foot slightly in front of the other.

3. Start the roll. Lean down, tuck your chin, and imagine curling up into a ball as you fall forward. Place your hands on the floor in front of you as you encounter the ground.

4. Roll over. Keep leaning forward, curling up as you go and keep your back curved as you contact the ground on the wide part of your back between your shoulder blades. If any part of your head touches the ground, you haven't curled up enough. If the ground hits you on the back with a thump, then you probably didn't lean down far enough.

5. Follow through. Try to maintain your momentum and roll up onto your feet.

Repeat steps 2 through 5 until you can smoothly roll up onto your feet every time.

Like all gymnastics, somersaulting takes some practice. Part of what you are learning is to flip upside down and not get all discombobulated. Discombobulation comes from confusion in your vestibular system, a group of internal organs and parts of your brain that help you keep track of what is up and what is down.

Once you have a good somersault technique, try doing two or three in a row and see what your vestibular system thinks of that. If that's not enough to discombobulate you, try doing it with your eyes closed.

PROGRESS

Date: ___ / ___ / ___   I did it! ☐

www.fiftydangerousthings.com/topic/03

COOTIES

SLAP

EMBARRASS-MENT

REQUIRES

☐ Another Person

DURATION   **DIFFICULTY**

WARNING

Always get permission before kissing someone.

Supplementary Data

The handshake can be traced back to more primitive times when it was customary to open your hands when meeting a stranger. An open hand can't conceal a weapon – a detail that might be very important when neither of you speak the same language.

Animal behaviorists see remarkable similarities when comparing the way adult humans greet each other to greeting behaviors in apes, monkeys, and dogs. Just as it is common for the lead dog (referred to as the "alpha") in a pack to physically dominate a newcomer, adult humans (especially males) often try to out-squeeze the other person in a handshake.

The distance that a person keeps between themselves and those around them is called "personal space". North Americans have some of the highest average personal space requirements on the planet.

HOW-TO

Typically this type of greeting is used in casual situations, but not in formal business situations.

1. Find someone who is willing to practice with you.

2. Stand two steps apart.

3. Say "Bonjour!" and step towards each other.

4. Put your right hand on their left shoulder.

5. Tilt your head slightly to the right and lean in so that your left cheek touches their left cheek.

6. Make a kiss noise with your lips, or turn your head slightly and kiss the other person's cheek.

7. Lean back.

8. Tilt your head slightly to the left and lean in so that your right cheek touches their right cheek.

9. Make a kiss noise with your lips, or turn your head slightly and kiss the other person's cheek.

In France, and much of Europe, this kind of greeting is common between friends and new acquaintances alike, but Americans are often confused and embarrassed the first few times they are greeted this way.

Embarrassment is recognized as having two main sources: personal, where we feel exposed in some manner, and professional, where our skills or knowledge are challenged. Developing a sense of humor helps us deal with embarrassments as they happen, a process sometimes referred to as "laughing it off." Learn to laugh off your embarrassments and you will develop confidence.

05 Stick Your Hand out the Window
Feel the air like a bird does

AMPUTATION

BROKEN BONES

REQUIRES

☐ Moving Vehicle (with openable window)
☐ Open Road

DURATION   **DIFFICULTY**

WARNING

Do not put your arm out if there is gravel or debris on the road. Make sure the car stays in the right-most lane so that no traffic will pass by your outstretched arm. Lock the door before you start. Finally, make sure your hand won't hit anything (mailboxes, tree branches, etc.) when you stick it out the window.

HOW-TO

1. Prepare. Enter the car and sit on the passenger side, then wait until you are traveling on an open stretch of road. Check the speed - 40 mph is a good speed to start with. Lower the window.

2. Reach out. With fingers together and palm facing down, slowly extend your arm until you can feel the air flowing over and under your hand. You may have to reach past the rear-view mirror if you are in the front seat.

3. Find the lift. Slowly rotate your hand up and down until you feel the wind lift the weight of your arm. Open and close your hand to feel what happens to the lift.

4. Experiment. Spread your fingers out - does that make more or less lift than having your fingers pressed together? Can you orient your hand to make the wind push it down? Where around the window is the wind the strongest and where is it weakest?

Air is all around us, squeezing us at a pressure of up to seven pounds per square inch (at sea level), yet we are so used to walking through it we hardly ever notice it.

Supplementary Data

Wind tunnels were invented almost 300 years ago to test airfoils. The wing being studied could be held still while the air was pushed past it to evaluate how well it flew (or didn't). This basic approach has enabled testing the aerodynamics of all manner of vehicles and buildings.

Vertical wind tunnels are used to simulate skydiving indoors.

Skyscrapers are designed to handle three kinds of load (or force): dead-load is the weight of the building itself, live-load is the weight of the things inside the building, and wind-load is the force of the wind pushing on the sides of the building. For tall skyscrapers the wind-load is the largest load.

The highest wind speed recorded on Earth is 231 mph. Wind speeds on Jupiter are calculated to exceed 385 mph.

Wind resistance is a significant factor in fuel efficiency. Almost half the fuel a car consumes is spent pushing air out of the way.

PROGRESS

Date: ___ / ___ / ___   I did it! ☐

www.fiftydangerousthings.com/topic/05

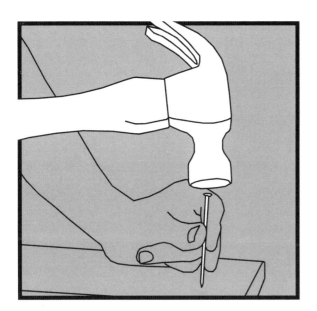

LOSE AN EYE

FRUSTRATION

CUTS AND SCRAPES

REQUIRES

- ☐ Hammer
- ☐ Nails (6d or two-inch)
- ☐ Board (soft pine or fir)
- ☐ Safety Goggles

DURATION   **DIFFICULTY**

WARNING

A poorly hit nail can fly up unpredictably; always wear eye protection.

Supplementary Data

In the United States nails are still described by the "penny", a system created back in England about 500 years ago – long before the United States existed. At that time "penny" was abbreviated "d" based on a Roman coin similar to a penny. The size indicated how much you paid for a hundred nails. Nowadays, a chart at the hardware store will tell you that a 6 penny nail is a two inch nail. The rest of the world, including England, now describes their nails in terms of length and diameter in millimeters.

A nail is a quick, strong way to put two pieces of wood together; a screw has the benefit of being easily removable. Professional house-builders usually prefer to use nails because they can be faster to use and are less expensive than screws.

Blacksmiths used to make nails by hand in a forge. These days, collectors rescue antique nails from old barns and houses. Some old nails have distinctive features that can be traced back to a specific blacksmith.

HOW-TO

Pounding nails can be very frustrating at first, especially after you accidentally hit your fingers a few times. Take your time and don't rush.

1. Prepare. Find a flat place to work where you won't have to worry about damaging the surface you are working on. The sidewalk is best, since a nail could go through the board and damage whatever is underneath.

2. Gather your materials. Many lumber stores give away scrap wood. Use a solid board at least ½ inch thick, and not made of particles or chips of wood. Keep your bag of nails handy.

3. Put on goggles.

4. Get a grip. Find the balance point on the hammer where it tips neither forward nor backward, and then slide your hand back just a little bit on the handle so that the head wants to tip down. Hold it firmly, but keep your wrist and arm relaxed.

5. Set the nail. Pinch it firmly between thumb and forefinger, with the pointed end on the board. Tap the head of the nail gently, so that it sticks in the board enough to stand on its own. Release the nail and brace the board with your hand.

6. Pound it. Continue to hit the nail with the hammer, increasing the force of the blows until the nail starts to visibly sink into the board.

Practice hammering until the tap-tap-tap of setting the nail transitions smoothly into the pound-pound-pound of driving the nail into the board. Try nailing two boards together, then make a stool that you can sit on.

PROGRESS

Date: ___ / ___ / ___   I did it! ☐

www.fiftydangerousthings.com/topic/06

COLLISION

PROPERTY DAMAGE

REQUIRES

☐ Car
☐ Empty Parking Lot
☐ Adult

DURATION

DIFFICULTY

WARNING

Keep your speed down and stay far away from any obstacles. Stop the car immediately if other cars or pedestrians enter the parking lot.

Supplementary Data

It is perfectly legal for a child to steer a car as long as it is on private property.

Driving on public roads is a privilege that is granted to a person by the state when they issue a license. Unlike your constitutional rights (free speech, freedom of religion, etc.), which can never be taken away from you, the state can take your driver license away if you behave irresponsibly in a car.

Driving on a road, with other cars, has more potential for danger than any of the activities in this book.

HOW-TO

Driving a car is serious business. Show that you are ready for the experience by paying attention when other people are driving.

1. Pick your location. Find an empty parking lot or open, flat field. Fewer obstacles means fewer opportunities for collisions. Have the adult drive the car to a spot where there is nothing in front of the car for as far as possible and turn off the engine.

2. Get behind the wheel. The adult will have to work the pedal and levers, so have them slide their seat back to make a space on their lap for you to sit. Make sure that they can still safely reach the steering wheel in case they need to take control. Review with them which of the controls you are and are not allowed to touch.

3. Prepare. Have the adult start the car and put it in drive, but ask them to keep their foot on the brake. You are about to take control; relax and take a deep breath. When you are ready, ask the adult to remove their foot from the brake and to apply a little gas.

4. Learn to steer. As the car rolls slowly forward, make small turns with the steering wheel so that the car weaves gently along your route. This will help you get a feel for how the car responds to the steering wheel.

5. Drive. When you are ready, pick a point ahead where there is a street light, lane marking, or concrete curb and plan to turn right or left around it. Keep planning and making turns until you can reliably turn the car when you want to and have it go where you mean it to. If there are lane markings, try staying in your lane when you make a turn.

Make up little driving goals and then try to do them. For example, in a parking lot with regular street lights, you could say "I'm going to drive in between the light poles."

Throw a Spear
Activate your built-in brain wiring

IMPALEMENT

DANGER TO OTHERS

CUTS AND SCRAPES

REQUIRES

☐ Straight Stick
☐ Clear Area (without people, pets or things that might get damaged)

DURATION

DIFFICULTY

WARNING

Find a place to practice where you won't be surprised by people accidentally walking into your target area. Make sure the shaft of your spear is smooth enough to hold and won't give you splinters.

```
Supplementary Data

The oldest wooden spears found were
400,000 years old.  However, wood does
not last forever, and some scientists
think that early humans may have used
spears as long as five million years
ago.

Andreas Thorkildsen threw a javelin
(a kind of spear) 297 feet to win the
gold medal and set a new world record
during the 2008 Summer Olympics.

The Aztecs used a device called an
atlatl ("aht-laht-l"), basically a
stick with a cupped end, to increase
the speed of a thrown spear to over
100 miles per hour.
```

HOW-TO

Almost any straight length of material will work as a spear if it is rigid enough. Look for a broomstick, piece of plastic pipe, or stick that is a little longer than you are tall. It's better to have it too long than too short, although you have to be able to lift and throw it with one hand, so not too heavy either.

1. Figure out the grip. Find the balance point of the spear where you can hold it in your open hand and it won't tip either forward or back. Then make sure you can grip it securely at that point.

2. Throw it. Hold the spear even with your ear. Take three quick steps, plant the foot opposite your spear hand, and then throw the spear as your body pivots over your planted foot.

3. Practice. Pick a spot on the ground and call it your target. Start as close as you need so that you can hit the target reliably, then take a few steps back. As soon as you can hit the target reliably, step back again.

The spear was quite likely one of the earliest technological innovations. First we had the rock, then someone threw a stick: instead of tumbling end-over-end, it flew straight and stuck in the ground - voila! This important moment in the history of human civilization has been lost in the sands of time, but it still stands as proof of the value of fooling around with stuff.

PROGRESS

Date: ___ / ___ / ___   I did it! ☐

www.fiftydangerousthings.com/topic/08

MAKE A MESS

LOSE AN EYE

PROPERTY DAMAGE

REQUIRES

- ☐ Resealable Plastic Bags (small)
- ☐ Measuring Spoons and Cups
- ☐ Baking Soda
- ☐ Vinegar
- ☐ Hot Water
- ☐ Paper Towel
- ☐ Safety Goggles

DURATION **DIFFICULTY**

WARNING

Explosions can throw material in random directions. Wear goggles or glasses to protect your eyes. Vinegar and baking soda can bleach certain materials and fabrics, so it's best to do this outside or in a bathtub.

HOW-TO

The trick is to get the two reactive compounds into the bag without letting them touch each other until after the bag is sealed.

1. Prepare reactant. Place two tablespoons of baking soda in the center of a paper towel and fold it up to make a sealed packet about 1½ inches square.

2. Prepare acid pool. Open the plastic bag and pour in ½ cup of vinegar and ¼ cup of hot water. The hot water helps the reaction go faster, resulting in a bigger explosion.

3. Assemble. Slip the packet down the inside of the plastic bag, being careful not to let it touch the pool of vinegar, and hold it in place while you seal the plastic bag closed.

4. Release. Toss the packet and stand back.

If your bag does not explode after you throw it, it's time to examine the results and determine why. Did the bag just stretch instead of pop? Did all of the baking soda get wet or did the packet stay closed and prevent the vinegar from reaching it? Did all of the baking soda get dissolved?

Because the acidity of vinegar varies widely from one manufacturer to another, you may have to play with the ratio of baking soda to vinegar to water until you discover the formula that works with your ingredients.

Supplementary Data

Baking soda reacts with the acid in vinegar to release carbon dioxide, one of the components of the air we breathe. The reaction is endothermic, meaning that as the reaction proceeds it draws energy from the environment – which is why we add hot water. Exothermic reactions like fire, firecrackers, and safety flares produce heat.

While the use of chemistry can be traced back 4000 years to the Egyptians, it wasn't until the end of the 1700s that a solid scientific basis was fully established. In 1783, Antoine Lavoisier was the first person to propose that when two compounds (like baking soda and vinegar) react, there is no new material created – only new combinations of the elements in the compounds. This idea became known as the theory of Conservation of Mass. This concept displaced some earlier notions that involved mysterious and invisible forces, and sparked a revolution in thinking that lead to the modern age of chemistry.

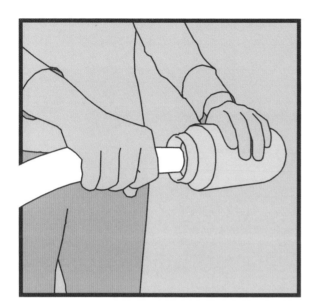

ANNOYING NOISE

HICKEY

LOSE AN EYE

REQUIRES

- ☐ Wide Mouth Jar
- ☐ Strips of Paper
- ☐ Ping Pong Ball
- ☐ Vacuum Cleaner
- ☐ Clean Filter/Bag

DURATION

DIFFICULTY

WARNING

Never let the end of the vacuum cleaner hose get near your face. Besides being dirty, the intense suction could do serious damage to your eyes.

Supplementary Data

Vacuum cleaners don't actually suck air. You can't actually pull on air, so a fan pushes air down the outflow tube, which lowers the pressure in the inflow tube. Atmospheric pressure then pushes air up the inflow tube to try and bring the pressure back up to normal.

Truck drivers use big nylon straps to tie down large loads on flatbed trucks. If you look closely at a passing truck you will see that they always put a twist in the straps so that they don't flap in the wind.

HOW-TO

Before you do any experiments with the vacuum cleaner, it's a good idea to change the bag or filter. Playing with the vacuum cleaner is an opportunity to discover things for yourself, but here are a couple of activities to get you started.

The Siren Jar

1. Remove the lid from a jar. The mouth of the jar must be bigger than the end of the vacuum cleaner hose, but not too much bigger.

2. Turn the vacuum cleaner on and insert the hose in the jar.

3. Keeping the hose in the center of the opening, slowly bring it out until it is just even with the top of the jar. If you explore this region you will find a spot where there is a very loud tone.

The Buzz Ribbon

1. Cut a strip of paper that is about ½ the width of the vacuum cleaner hose and up to 12 inches long.

2. Turn the vacuum cleaner on.

3. Hold one end of the paper strip and let the vacuum cleaner begin to suck the other end of the strip into the hose. Hang on tightly to the strip and let more of it into the hose until it begins to buzz. Where is the sound the loudest?

The Floating Ball

1. Connect the hose to the outflow side of the vacuum cleaner. Note that not all vacuum cleaners have this feature.

2. Turn the vacuum cleaner on and hold the end of the hose so that it points straight up.

3. Release a ping pong ball into the upward jet of air. If it just shoots up and falls off to the side, try partially covering the intake on the vacuum cleaner so that less air comes out the outflow hose.

PROGRESS

Date: ___ / ___ / ___   I did it! ☐

www.fiftydangerousthings.com/topic/10

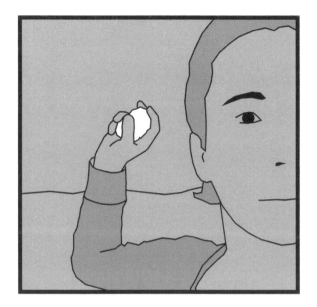

BUMPS AND BRUISES

DANGER TO OTHERS

PROPERTY DAMAGE

REQUIRES

☐ Rocks
☐ Clear Area (without people, pets or things that might get damaged)

DURATION   **DIFFICULTY**

WARNING

Never throw a rock where you can't see it land. Never throw rocks where people or animals might appear unexpectedly. Every rock you pick up, you become responsible for.

Supplementary Data

You can get better at throwing rocks even if you are lying in your bed at night. Researchers have shown that we can improve skills by imagining doing them - almost as much as by actually doing them! Close your eyes and imagine, as clearly as you can, picking up a rock, feeling the weight in your hand, and throwing it at the target.

The path of a rock through the air traces a curve described by mathematicians as a parabola. The curve is the cumulative result of the effects of gravity and wind resistance. If you were in outer space, the rocks you threw would travel in straight lines - practically forever.

Geologists recognize three basic types of rock: igneous, sedimentary and metamorphic. Igneous means "born of fire" and is used to describe rocks formed by magma.

HOW-TO

Throwing rocks takes practice. At first the motion of throwing can feel awkward, but if you keep doing it you will find that it becomes natural.

1. Prepare. Find a place where you have some room to throw as hard as you want and collect some suitable rocks. Look for rocks that are about as big as the circle created by your thumb and forefinger when you make the 'OK' sign.

2. Make a target. Almost anything will work, but an empty soda can or a piece of cardboard on a stick about chest-high will provide good feedback for accurate tosses.

3. Aim. Stand about 10 paces away from the target. Hold a rock lightly but firmly, cradling it between your thumb and first two fingers. Then, look at the target and do not take your eyes off of the target while throwing.

4. Throw the rock. Observe the path of the rock and notice whether it passes above or below the target. Don't worry too much about hitting the target right away, you need to develop a good solid throw before you can aim reliably.

When you can hit the target reliably from 10 paces, take two steps backward and throw from there. Repeat until you can hit the target from 20 paces.

There are many little tricks and techniques that will improve your throwing ability. Most of them you will discover by spending time throwing rocks, others you will have to seek out.

Pay attention whenever you see someone throwing a ball; notice how they plant their feet, notice how they hold the ball. These little details can make large improvements in your ability to accurately throw a rock.

PROGRESS

Date: ___ / ___ / ___   I did it! ☐

www.fiftydangerousthings.com/topic/11

BURNS

PROJECTILES

LOSE AN EYE

REQUIRES

☐ Dry Ice
☐ Towel, Pie Plate, Cup, Plastic Fork
☐ Water
☐ Safety Goggles
☐ Hammer

DURATION

DIFFICULTY

WARNING

Dry ice is extremely cold - much colder than regular ice or even your freezer. Prolonged contact with skin can cause painful frostbite injuries (similar to a burn). Always use a dry towel or oven mitts to move or hold the block of ice, and protect your eyes when working with it. Never put dry ice in your mouth.

HOW-TO

As with all play activities, you should explore your own ideas - always observing the safe-handling rules, of course. Here are some ideas to get you started.

Breaking Up Dry Ice

1. Carefully wrap the block of dry ice in a towel.
2. Put on goggles.
3. Whack the wrapped block with a hammer until it breaks up into pieces. Save some large pieces that you can break up later because the small pieces will evaporate very quickly.

Ice Scooters

1. Half-fill a pie plate with water and set on table.
2. Using a fork, drop small pieces of dry ice onto the surface of the water.

Boiling Cup of Fog

1. Put one drop of water in the bottom of a cup.
2. Drop a flake of dry ice into the cup and use the fork to nudge it into the water. With a little practice, you can get the water to freeze the flake to the bottom of the cup.
3. Slowly fill cup halfway with water so that you don't dislodge the flake and it stays stuck to the bottom of the cup.

Supplementary Data

Dry ice, which is frozen carbon dioxide, does not melt, it goes directly from solid to gas in a process called sublimation. At normal atmospheric pressure, carbon dioxide has no liquid form. Water will also slowly sublimate if the temperature and humidity are low enough – this is why ice cubes in the freezer shrink.

Water freezes at 32°F, but carbon dioxide does not freeze until -109°F. Organisms which can survive in harsh conditions are collectively referred to as extremophiles, but the ones that can survive in extreme cold are specifically called cryophiles. The existence of cryophiles on Earth makes astrobiologists wonder if there could be life on some of the icy moons in our solar system.

Dry ice is sold in some grocery stores, and many ice companies sell it directly to the public.

What else does dry ice want to do?

PROGRESS

Date: ___ / ___ / ___   I did it! ☐

www.fiftydangerousthings.com/topic/12

BURNS

FIRE

SMOKE DETECTOR

REQUIRES

☐ Stove
☐ Paper Cup (unwaxed)
☐ Water

DURATION   **DIFFICULTY**

WARNING

Boiling water is very hot, and a paper cup full of it is a tricky thing to deal with. It may be safer to keep boiling until all the water has evaporated, rather than to try and move the cup once you start.

HOW-TO

It's very important that the paper cup not be plastic coated, and that it have a flat bottom. If you can't find a simple paper cup, you can make an origami box (search: masu). Using wax paper is OK. Use a gas or electric stove; an inductive cooktop won't work.

1. Make a plan. Before you turn the stove on, figure out where over the burner the cup likes to sit. The cup needs to be stable, not tippy, and upright. It also must be directly on the flame or heat coil to get very hot. If the grate does not support the cup very well, a piece of metal screen can be placed over the grate to make a stable platform.

2. Prepare. Fill cup with water so it is about ¾ full and place on burner where it will be hottest (over the flame or on heat coil).

3. Heat. Turn burner on high. We use high to heat it quickly, because the paper can fall apart if it gets too soggy.

4. Wait for water to boil. It is normal for the top edge of the cup, above the water line, to turn brown and possibly even ignite because the water is not keeping it cool. Do not be alarmed. As the water boils away, the cup will get shorter as it burns away.

Now you have a burning, boiling, cup of water on the stove - how will you get it off of there? Here are a couple of options: boil away the water until only a piece of wet paper is left; use a spatula to tip the cup into a pan; turn off the stove and wait until cool.

Supplementary Data

The exact temperature at which water boils depends on atmospheric pressure. At 3300ft water will start to boil at 206°F - a full 6°F lower than at sea level - much to the consternation of cooks. Water boils at 212°F (or less) but paper doesn't burn until it gets to almost 500°F.

Under most circumstances, you can't raise the temperature of water past 212°F because steam is produced at exactly the rate necessary to carry heat energy away from the water so that the temperature never gets above boiling (a process referred to as "enthalpy of transformation"). Since the boiling temperature is so far below the ignition temperature of paper and wood, water is used to put out many types of fires.

However, water and other liquids can be "superheated" in a microwave. In this rare situation, surface-tension suppresses the normal formation of bubbles as the water is being heated. The result is a dangerous condition that can cause a flash-boil if the container is bumped or stirred.

Gas stoves are adaptable to burn either propane or natural gas. While both gases burn at about 1093°F, propane is more than twice as efficient when compared by volume.

PROGRESS

Date: ___ / ___ / ___   I did it! ☐

www.fiftydangerousthings.com/topic/13

FIRE

BAD STINK

BURNS

REQUIRES

☐ Microwave Oven
☐ Grapes (or grape tomatoes)
☐ Unwanted CD
☐ Marshmallows

DURATION   **DIFFICULTY**

WARNING

Before we start putting things in the microwave, there are a couple of rules we must follow in order to minimize the danger to ourselves and the microwave.

10 Second Limit - never power any experiment for more than 10 seconds at a time.

Cancel and Contain - if the experiment should happen to catch fire, immediately hit the 'Cancel' or 'Stop' button, and keep the door closed until the fire goes out.

Expect it to be Hot - small objects that absorb microwave energy have a tendency to heat up, sometimes spectacularly. Use an oven mitt or tongs when removing experiments from the microwave.

> **Supplementary Data**
>
> Microwave ovens occasionally have dead spots. If any of your experiments fail to produce interesting results, try repeating it in different locations within the oven.

HOW-TO

Metal Foil

A CD is just a thin sheet of aluminum foil sealed between circular sheets of hard plastic. Microwaves are absorbed by metal (that's why you are never supposed to put cutlery in the microwave) and when the metal is thin enough, surprising things can happen.

1. Place an unwanted CD on a paper towel in the microwave.

2. Run at full power for 3 seconds.

The Grape Antenna

All radio wave lengths can be measured as the distance between peaks in the waveform. As it turns out, a common grape is about one-quarter of the wavelength of the energy produced in a microwave oven - a magical relationship for highly efficient antennas.

1. Cut a grape almost in half, leaving the skin as a hinge between the two halves.

2. Place the grape, open faces up, on a microwave-safe plate.

3. Run at full power for 10 seconds.

Marshmallow Fluff

Besides being sweet, marshmallows have a couple of properties that make them perfectly suited to microwave experiments: they are fluffy, stretchy, and moist. The water content helps them absorb microwaves, the trapped air makes them heat quickly, and the taffy-like consistency means that they can expand stupendously.

1. Place a marshmallow on a microwave-safe plate in the oven.

2. Run at full power for 10 seconds.

A microwave oven is really a high-energy physics laboratory that we use every day. What will you try next?

15 Throw Things from a Moving Car
Play with speed, gravity, and wind resistance

GET A TICKET

AMPUTATION

BROKEN BONES

REQUIRES

- [ ] Moving Vehicle (with openable window)
- [ ] Open Road
- [ ] Water Balloon
- [ ] Whole Orange
- [ ] Squirt Gun
- [ ] Banana

DURATION

DIFFICULTY

WARNING

The impact velocity of an object thrown from a moving car meeting a car traveling in the opposite direction can exceed 100 mph; therefore we must be extra careful. Never throw objects when there are any other cars around. Never throw objects when there is a chance of them hitting a person or private property. Note that it is illegal in many places to throw anything from a moving vehicle - check local laws and act responsibly.

HOW-TO

The list of suggested items to use for this activity is just that: a suggestion. You may think of other things to try, but keep in mind that whatever you throw from the car should not be litter or dangerous to other cars.

1. Prepare. Arrange to be sitting on the passenger side of a car traveling on an open stretch of road. Check the car's speed; 40 mph is perfect. Lower the window.

2. Predict. Hold the banana in your hand and imagine throwing it out the open window, directly away from the car. Describe where you think it will land.

3. Throw. Toss the banana away from the car. Did it land where you expected? Hold the orange in your hand and imagine throwing it forward (but not so that you end up driving over it). Describe where you think it will land. Throw the orange. Lean out a bit and drop the water balloon. How much road went by between the time you let go, and when the balloon hit the road?

4. Squirt. Keep a firm grip on the squirt gun and hold it out the window. See if you can hit the windshield with water from the squirt gun. How about the back window?

Suppose that you had to deliver eggs from a moving car. How could you package an egg so that it would survive being tossed from the car window?

> **Supplementary Data**
>
> The study of how objects behave in moving air is called aerodynamics. If you are studying moving water, then it's called hydrodynamics. And if you study electrically conductive fluids, it's called magnetohydrodynamics.
>
> In aerodynamics, "drag" is the term used to describe the air resistance on a moving car. At freeway speeds, drag is the largest factor in fuel efficiency. This is the primary reason that car designs get sleeker over time - it's not just to make them look fast.
>
> Of all the fish in the sea, the tuna is considered to have the least hydrodynamic drag.

PROGRESS

Date: ___ / ___ / ___   I did it! ☐

www.fiftydangerousthings.com/topic/15

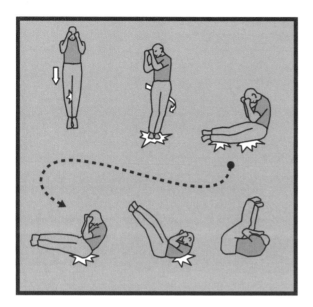

BUMPS AND BRUISES

FALL

SPRAINED ANKLE

REQUIRES

☐ Park Bench
☐ Sturdy Shoes (boots are best)

DURATION   **DIFFICULTY**

WARNING

The parachute landing fall, or PLF as it is commonly referred to, is only designed to minimize the injury when impacting the ground. Even done perfectly, the PLF will not prevent injury from high falls. Unless you have a giant pile of sawdust or straw, never attempt this from a height of more than about 18 inches.

```
Supplementary Data

The PLF was invented by the British
Army in the 1940s to distribute the
energy of paratrooper landing impact
to the largest muscle groups in your
body: peroneus longus (outside of
your calf), vastus lateralis (outer
thigh), gluteus maximus (buttock),
and the latissimus dorsi (side of
your back). Bending your legs makes
them act like shock absorbers, and
keeps the landing shock from being
transmitted directly to your spine.

Terminal velocity is the maximum speed
a free-falling object will attain in
Earth's atmosphere. Terminal velocity
for a skydiver is around 120 miles
per hour.
```

HOW-TO

Start on the ground and only move up to the bench when you feel all five contact points hit in the right sequence.

1. **Prepare.** Close your hands into fists and hold them in front of, and slightly to the side of, your face. Your elbows should be tucked in against your chest. Bend your knees slightly and press them together as if you were holding a sheet of paper between them. Tense the muscles in your legs. Look out at the horizon, not down at the ground.

2. **Jump!** If you are on the bench, hop off into the air. If you are starting on the ground, just hop up into the air. Point the balls of your feet at the ground, making sure to keep your ankles pressed together. Don't point your toes - they can get stubbed if you land on them.

3. **First contact.** As soon as the balls of your feet touch the ground, twist your upper body to the side (away from the bench). Keep your knees together and curl your upper body towards your feet, tucking your head against your chest.

4. **Second contact.** Feel the outside of your calf touch the ground.

5. **Third contact.** Let your body fall onto your thigh muscle.

6. **Fourth contact.** Continue the rolling motion across your buttocks, and as your legs lift into the air keep your knees together and slightly bent.

7. **Fifth contact.** Finish the roll by letting the side of your back hit the ground, and let the air out of your lungs with a big "Oof!"

Repeat until you can reliably and smoothly roll through all five contact points every time.

PROGRESS

Date: ___ / ___ / ___   I did it! ☐

www.fiftydangerousthings.com/topic/16

BURNS

FIRE

PROPERTY DAMAGE

REQUIRES

☐ Magnifying Glass (available at drug stores)
☐ Scratch Paper
☐ Fresh Fruit

DURATION   **DIFFICULTY**

WARNING

Anything that you ignite, you are responsible for extinguishing. Always work in a clear area where you can't accidentally ignite anything other than your intended material. Light hot enough to burn paper can also burn you - don't focus the light on anything that you don't intend to try to ignite.

HOW-TO

Treat the lens of the magnifying glass gently. The glass can be scratched easily, and each scratch reduces the effectiveness of the lens.

1. Prepare. Find or make an area cleared of flammable materials. A sidewalk, driveway, or dirt path are ideal.

2. Focus the light. Hold the lens above the paper and notice the bright circle of light that it makes. Move the lens up and down until you make the smallest circle of light - this is concentrated sunlight and it's very hot.

3. Burn. Hold the lens still and observe the effect on paper. Try the same procedure with fresh fruit.

Once you determine the proper height for the lens, you might want to make a little stand that will hold it there. A coat hanger bent into a tripod shape and a little tape can do that nicely.

The amount of heat you generate at the focal point of the lens depends on the size of the lens and the angle of the sun in the sky. The atmosphere absorbs and reflects some light. When the sun is low on the horizon, the light must travel through more of the atmosphere to reach you.

There are lots of interesting things you can do with a hot point of light. Try writing your name on a scrap of wood, or use the heat to melt a piece of plastic (but don't breathe the fumes). Experiment.

Supplementary Data

The speed of light is a constant - in a vacuum. Light travels at different speeds through different materials, so when it goes from one material to another (from air to glass) it changes direction in a predictable way. This phenomenon is called "refraction" and it's that change of direction that enables a lens to focus light or drops of water to make a rainbow.

It seems remarkable that anything is transparent. After all, glass is more dense than wood and yet somehow visible light can go right through it. Air, water, plastic, and certain minerals share this property, but are about the only substances transparent to visible light. However, as it turns out, everything is transparent to some form of electromagnetic radiation. Our bodies are transparent to x-rays, the planet is transparent to cosmic rays, and paper is transparent to microwaves.

Travelling at 186,000 miles per second, it takes the light from the Sun just over 8 minutes to reach the surface of the Earth.

TRAFFIC

WANDERLUST

WARNING

The most dangerous thing you are likely to encounter on a walk is a moving car. You must always assume that the cars are not watching out for you and that you are the only person who can get yourself across the street safely. You and your parent are the best judge of the relative safety of your community and must decide together if is safe to walk home after school.

HOW-TO

Before you can walk home, you must demonstrate that you can safely cross the street and use a cellphone. If you don't go to a school, or school is only a short distance away, pick a location at least ½ mile from home to walk to and back.

1. Prepare. Make a map of how you will get home, and make a mark at the halfway point on the journey. Check the charge on the cellphone, and test to make sure that you can call home quickly and easily.

2. Go to school.

3. Check your map and cellphone. Call home and let someone know that you are about to start walking. Estimate how long you think it will take you to get to the halfway point.

4. Start walking. Follow the route that you agreed on. If you get lost, use your map, ask for directions, or call home for advice. Check the time when you arrive at the halfway point - was your estimate accurate?

5. Arrive home. Safe and sound.

Once you're familiar with the route, you may not need to call home (or even carry a cellphone) when out walking.

Pay attention to the things you see as you walk home. Even if you are driven on the very same route every day, you will notice things that you never noticed from the car.

Supplementary Data

An adult walks at about 3 miles per hour, and can comfortably cover about 20 miles each day over even ground.

It usually takes people between six and eight months to walk across the United States, a distance of approximately 3000 miles. Doris Haddock was 89 when she decided to try it. She met terrible weather in the Appalachian Mountains, had to ski over 100 miles, and finally arrived in Washington D.C. when she was 92.

A pair of good running shoes should last between 300 and 500 miles before needing to be replaced.

Animals that walk on two legs are known as bipeds. Bipeds are either walkers like humans and birds, or hoppers like kangaroos and certain types of mice.

The only mode of transportation for a person that is more energy efficient than walking is riding a bicycle.

PROGRESS

Date: ___ / ___ / ___   I did it! ☐

www.fiftydangerousthings.com/topic/18

FALL

CUTS AND SCRAPES

PROPERTY DAMAGE

REQUIRES

☐ Ladder
☐ Roof Access
☐ Adult

DURATION   **DIFFICULTY**

WARNING

A fall from any height, even just a few inches, let alone roof-height, can result in very serious injuries. Plan where you are going on the roof and how you will get back, and then move slowly while you are up there.

Supplementary Data

Since the dawn of civilization, people have been inventing new ways to cover a roof. Before the advent of efficient transportation, roofing materials were made solely from local materials and often had to be replaced or repaired every season.

Slate is so durable it can last more than 200 years. Clay tiles have such a distinctive look that some communities actually require all houses to have them (such as Santa Barbara's historic district). However tile is often fragile and slippery so it's usually not good to climb on.

One of the newest - and oldest - roof coverings is grass. Sod roofs have been found in Scandinavia for centuries, but new technology is now creating "green" roofs such as Chicago's City Hall, one of the first in the US.

HOW-TO

Climbing a roof is not that much different from climbing a tree or boulder, in that falling from any of them can result in a bad injury. But buildings are designed to look tidy and do not offer as many clues about their stability and soundness as natural objects do. If the surface comes loose when you rub it with your fingers, it may be unsafe to walk on.

1. Find a good roof. Look for one that is not too steep, not more than one story above the ground, in good condition, and that you can get permission to climb.

2. Set the ladder. Determine the best place to get up on the roof and place the ladder there. The top of the ladder should be 3 feet above the edge of the roof. Make sure the ladder is stable and have an adult hold it while you go up.

3. Climb the ladder. Hold the rungs and not the sides as you go up. When you are holding the last rung, step on to the roof.

4. Climb the roof. Walk straight up to the peak, always keeping the top of the ladder directly below you in case you slide. Watch out for loose shingles or debris on the roof that might slide when you step on it.

5. Enjoy the view. Put one foot firmly on each side of the peak to keep you stable, and have a look around.

6. Climb down the roof. Walk straight down from the peak to the ladder, keeping your weight on your toes and not your heels. Grasp the top rung and then step around to get your feet onto the ladder.

7. Climb down the ladder. Watch where you place your feet and always face the ladder as you go down.

PROGRESS

Date: ___ / ___ / ___   I did it! ☐

www.fiftydangerousthings.com/topic/19

20 | Squash Pennies on a Railroad Track
Leverage the force of a locomotive

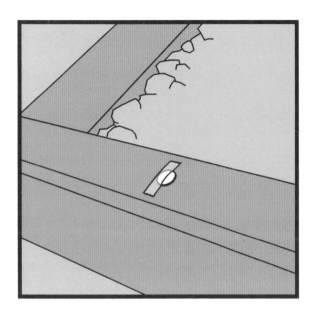

GET A TICKET

PROJECTILES

RUN OVER BY TRAIN

REQUIRES

☐ Pennies (or other coins)
☐ Tape
☐ Active Train Track
☐ Train Schedule

DURATION   **DIFFICULTY**

WARNING

Because of the unfamiliar size of train engines, our brains do not accurately judge the distance and speed of oncoming trains. If you see or hear a train, assume that it is a danger and move to a safe distance immediately.

Coins may squirt out from under train wheels, so stand at least 30 feet away from where you have placed your penny.

HOW-TO

1. Pick a location. Find a length of track that is actively used and very straight - you want to be able to see and hear the train coming from a long way away. The best location is next to an automated crossing gate - the bells will warn you when a train is coming.

2. Pick a moment. Check the schedule for a gap of at least 15 minutes between trains. Not all train traffic is scheduled, so you must still wait for a time when you can neither see nor hear any trains or crossing bells.

3. Place the penny. Tape the penny to the top of the rail. If there is a bright, shiny, part of the rail, tape the penny there - that's where the wheel will make the most contact. The tape will help prevent the vibration of the approaching train from shaking the penny off the rail before it gets squashed.

4. Mark the spot. Put a stick on the ground pointing at the place where you have taped the penny.

5. Stand back and wait. Stand at least 30 feet away from ALL tracks, and wait for a train to pass. If the tape does not hold the penny in place, it may come flying out at high velocity.

6. Find the penny. After the train passes, and you can neither see nor hear any trains or crossing bells, find the squashed penny. Be careful, it may still be hot from being squashed. Get away from the track as soon as you have your penny.

```
Supplementary Data
Trains have no steering wheel.

The faster you want a train to go,
the smoother the track has to be. If
the pieces of the track are bolted
together with plates then only slow
trains use it; if they are welded
into a continuous piece of rail, the
track is probably designed for faster
trains.

While a coin has never derailed a
train, more than one person has been
injured putting coins on a rail.
Usually, it's because they acciden-
tally stand on another track while
waiting, and a train comes down that
other track and hits them.
```

Using the tape, it may be possible to get two different types of coins to squash together. Preparing them by sanding the surfaces will increase the chances of a good metallurgical bond.

To ensure that you don't harm the train or the track, never put anything larger than a coin or two on the tracks.

PROGRESS

Date: ___ / ___ / ___   I did it! ☐

www.fiftydangerousthings.com/topic/20

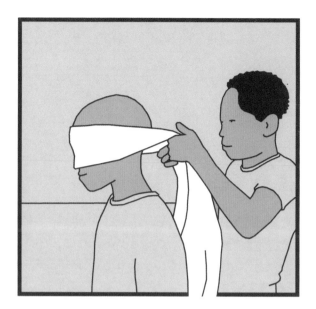

TRIP

FRUSTRATION

BUMPS AND BRUISES

REQUIRES

☐ Assistance
☐ Old T-shirt, Size L (or clean rags)
☐ Scissors

DURATION　　　　**DIFFICULTY**

WARNING

Once you are blindfolded, move cautiously. What would be a minor stumble with eyes open can become a cascade of collisions which may result in either laughter or tears. Your assistant should be prepared to intervene before you get into serious trouble.

Supplementary Data

There are many ways that blind people have learned to "see" their surroundings: a cane helps avoid obstacles and identify curbs, clickers help to hear the shape of the world, guide-dogs can assist with crossing streets and warn of unexpected dangers, and scientists are experimenting with brain implants that can provide new forms of sight.

Neuroscientists have proved that eyes are not necessary for seeing. One way uses a special chair connected to a camera. The chair "draws" the image on the sitter's back with four hundred vibrating squares. A blind person sitting in the chair is able to quickly learn to recognize objects placed in front of the camera.

HOW-TO

For this experience to work, you have to make a blindfold that prevents any light from reaching your eyes and wear it long enough for your brain to start relying on your other senses. Try wearing the blindfold for at least one hour.

1. Make a blindfold. Lay the t-shirt on the table and cut six inches off of the bottom to create a ring of material. Find the seam on the ring and cut along it to create a long rectangle of material - this is the primary part of your blindfold. Fold the rectangle along the long axis.

2. Make it dark. Cut two 8 inch squares of material from the remainder of the t-shirt. Fold the squares in half, and in half again, to make small eye patches. Gently place the blindfold over your eyes and tie it behind your head. Tuck the patches under the blindfold directly over your eyes. Adjust the blindfold and the patches until you cannot see any difference between light and dark.

3. Begin. Sit still for a few moments while you adjust to your new situation, then explore your surroundings.

Without consciously thinking about it, we maintain an internal model of the world around us and update it with information gleaned from what we see. This model is remarkably detailed, but take away sight and the model quickly becomes unreliable - until we learn to rely on our other senses.

5 Things to do while blindfolded:

1. Eat a meal.
2. Use the bathroom.
3. Go for a walk.
4. Try to catch a ball.
5. Draw a map of the room you are in.

How many more can you think of?

PROGRESS

Date: ___ / ___ / ___   I did it! ☐

www.fiftydangerousthings.com/topic/21

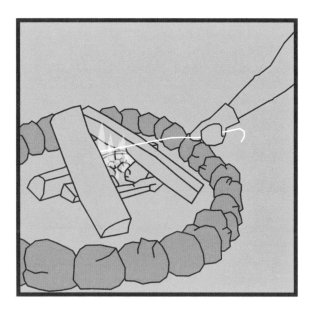

BURNS

FIRE

PROPERTY DAMAGE

REQUIRES

☐ Wire Coat Hanger (preferably uncoated)
☐ Fire (#45)
☐ Water Bucket
☐ Oven Mitts
☐ Adult Supervision

DURATION

DIFFICULTY

WARNING

Any time you heat up a piece of metal there is a possibility that someone will get hurt. Always wear the oven mitts when handling the wire, and never set it down until you know it is cool enough to not hurt anyone or set fire to anything.

HOW-TO

You will need a good, hot fire for this project. Get one started early and wait until some coals have formed.

1. Prepare. Fill a bucket with water and set it next to your fire. Unwind the hook, and separate the two ends of the coat hanger. Straighten the wire a bit. It doesn't have to be perfectly straight, just kind of straight. Notice how hard it is to straighten the tight bends even a little.

2. Heat the wire. Put on oven mitts and place the middle of the wire in the hottest part of the fire, making sure neither end of the wire is getting heated - so you'll have something to hold on to later. Leave the wire in the fire until it glows orange.

3. Bend it. With the oven mitts on, pick up the wire. Being careful to only touch the unheated ends, try to make the wire bend where it is glowing. If it won't bend easily, put it back in the fire. Quench the hot bend by plunging it into the water.

By repeated heating and bending, you may be able to make all manner of shapes. This process works on metal of any size: from tiny wires to railroad track. If you had a hammer, an anvil, and some goggles, you could pound the red hot wire into a flat sheet of steel.

Perhaps only Superman can bend cold steel with his bare hands, but once you understand the properties of your materials and how they can be changed, you can create anything.

Supplementary Data

Pots rarely turn red-hot on a stove because they dissipate heat much more effectively than the wire does.

Quenching makes some metals stronger because it prevents crystalline structures from forming at the atomic level. Slow cooling allows those structures to form - which can make metals harder, but also more brittle.

Materials scientists describe metals in terms of ductility and malleability: terms that describe how easily a metal can be stretched and pounded.

Steel is an alloy usually made from iron mixed with carbon, although other elements such as tungsten and manganese are also used. The inclusion of other elements results in a harder, more rust-resistant material than pure iron.

Archeologists divide the history of most ancient civilizations into three general periods: the Stone Age, when the people start to use tools made from rocks; the Bronze Age, when they first discover the simple metals; and the Iron Age, when they smelt and use iron to create steel.

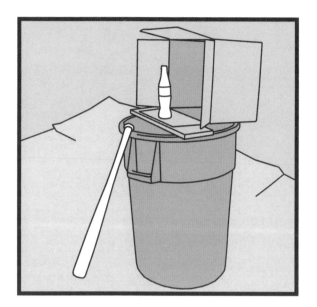

PROJECTILES

MAKE A MESS

CUTS AND SCRAPES

REQUIRES

☐ Large Empty Garbage Can
☐ Large Cardboard Box
☐ Empty Glass Bottles
☐ Wood Board
☐ Bat or Metal Pipe
☐ Safety Goggles
☐ Long Sleeved Shirt or Jacket
☐ Gloves
☐ Broom and Dustpan
☐ Tape

DURATION

DIFFICULTY

WARNING

Broken glass can be very sharp. Wear goggles and long sleeves when bashing bottles with a baseball bat. Have gloves, a broom and a dust-pan handy for cleanup.

HOW-TO

There are going to be sharp bits of glass flying around, so make sure everyone, including the spectators, wears goggles and long sleeved shirts.

1. Setup. Place a board across the top of an empty garbage can. Create a glass-catcher by taping a cardboard box to the board. Fold the box flaps back so that they fan out away from the box to act as shields.

2. Prepare your target. Place an empty bottle in the center of the board, on top of the flap, as shown in the diagram.

3. Batter up. Put on goggles and take a swing at the bottle with a bat. Try to hit the bottle so that the box will catch the broken glass. If the bottle falls into the garbage can without breaking, wear gloves when you reach in to retrieve it.

Alternative setup:

1. Drop a bottle into an empty garbage can.

2. Throw other bottles at it until one of them breaks.

Sometimes it just feels good to break something. That feeling doesn't make you a bad person, unless you go around deliberately breaking things all the time. Psychologists who study how the mind works use the term "cathartic" to describe activities that relieve mental stress.

Supplementary Data

The sharpest knives in the world are made from broken obsidian, a type of naturally occurring volcanic glass. Native Americans had been making spearheads and knives from obsidian for thousands of years before modern science rediscovered the technique and started using it again. Biologists and surgeons covet the blades because the sharp edges can be as little as one-molecule thick: thin enough to cut between the cells of a person or plant.

The windshields of cars are made of laminated safety glass. A windshield is really two sheets of glass with a layer of very strong plastic sandwiched between them. The glass is designed to break into very small pieces and the plastic is designed to hang on to the fragments. This reduces the danger posed by broken window glass when there is an accident.

PROGRESS

Date: ___ / ___ / ___   I did it! ☐

www.fiftydangerousthings.com/topic/23

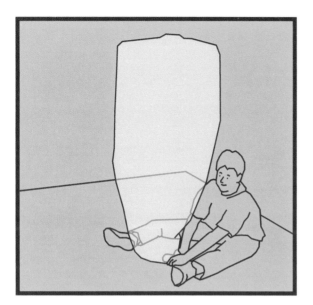

BURNS

FRUSTRATION

REQUIRES

☐ Dry Cleaner Bag (not torn)
☐ Blow Dryer
☐ Scissors
☐ Transparent Tape
☐ One Penny

DURATION

DIFFICULTY

WARNING

Don't run with scissors, don't use the blow dryer in the bathtub, and don't stick anything other than a power plug into an electrical outlet.

Supplementary Data

You would think that a blow dryer would be a pretty safe household appliance by now - after all, it's been around for decades. But did you know that there are thousands of blow dryer related injuries reported every year? Is there something inherently dangerous about blow dryers? Or could it just be that blow dryers are typically used in the bathroom: the site of more than half of all household accidents?

This is an example of what statisticians refer to as "masking." The environment of the bathroom is so accident-prone that blow dryers get a bad reputation, when in fact they may be no more dangerous than can-openers.

Hot-air balloons carry their own sources of heat in the form of large propane burners that the pilot can control. The pilot is called a "balloonist."

HOW-TO

Hot air is lighter than cold air, and that difference can be enough to make a bag fly.

1. Remove excess weight. Trim any excess material from around the seams at the top of a dry cleaner bag (the top is the end where the coat hanger would go). The less the bag weighs, the more it will want to fly.

2. Using as little tape as possible, seal any little holes that you find in the sides of the bag. Every bit of tape adds weight.

3. Align the bottom edges of the bag and seal with tape, but leave the last 2 inches at each end of the seam open. One opening is for the blow dryer (providing hot air), the other is to let the cold air out of the bag.

4. Spread the bag out so that it can inflate without having to unfold. You may want to put down a cloth to lay the bag on, so that the bag doesn't accidentally get torn.

5. Insert the end of the blow dryer into one of the holes in the bag and turn it on. If it has separate controls for heat and speed, you probably want the hottest temperature and the lowest speed (so that the bag fills gently and doesn't tear).

6. As the bag inflates, lift the top so that the hot air has a place to go and the cold air inside the bag can fall out. Continue to inflate until the bag lifts off.

If the bag wants to fly upside down, see if there is any more material on the top that can be removed without making a hole. If that doesn't work, try taping the penny to the bottom of the bag.

PROGRESS

Date: ___ / ___ / ___   I did it! ☐

www.fiftydangerousthings.com/topic/24

GO BLIND

FIRE

- ☐ Binoculars
- ☐ Cardboard
- ☐ Blank Sheet of White Paper
- ☐ Tape
- ☐ Utility Knife
- ☐ Friend (extra hands will be helpful)

DURATION   **DIFFICULTY**

WARNING

Never look directly at the sun - even a brief glimpse of the sun through binoculars can cause permanent eye injury. Avoid igniting the viewing paper by making sure that the image of the sun doesn't get too small.

HOW-TO

Our Sun is the source of all life on Earth, yet we spend our lives avoiding looking directly at it because of the damage it can do to our eyes. You have to build something to get a good look at the sun.

1. Make a shade. Measure and cut holes in the center of a piece of cardboard to fit tightly around the wide ends of the binoculars. Push the binoculars through the holes and cover any little gaps between the binoculars and cardboard with tape. (Blue painter's tape is removed most easily from the binoculars after you are done.)

2. Align the viewer. Hold the binoculars above a sheet of plain white paper and angle the large end of the binoculars towards the sun. A bright white spot will appear on the paper when you are lined up. Pull the binoculars away from the paper until the spot grows to the size of an orange.

3. Focus. Adjust the focus on the binoculars until the edges of the spot are sharp. You might want to enlist a friend to help: one of you holds the binoculars in position while the other adjusts the focus knob.

If you look closely at the projected image of the sun, you may see a few dark spots. Those are sunspots. They appear dark because a twisting column of intense magnetic energy is holding open a hole on the surface of the sun.

> **Supplementary Data**
>
> A typical sunspot is three times as wide as the Earth.
>
> Sunspots vary over time - sometimes there are many active spots and other times there are none.
>
> The surface of our Sun is approximately 9950°F. Based on its color and temperature, astronomers classify it as a type G2V star and yellow dwarf.
>
> Most of the stars in the universe are red dwarfs, but we are lucky to have a healthy star with enough hydrogen to fuel it for another 5 billion years before it starts to change - despite the fact that it uses up 4 million tons of the stuff every second.
>
> Everything on Earth, and everywhere else in the Universe, was made from material that came from stars like the Sun. In a very real sense, we are all made of stars.
>
> Scientists estimate that the light from the Sun that reaches the Earth delivers about twice as much energy in just one year as we will ever get from all of the oil, coal, natural gas, and mined uranium used by human-kind.

PROGRESS

Date: ___ / ___ / ___   I did it! ☐

www.fiftydangerousthings.com/topic/25

Learn Dramatic Sword Fighting
A behind-the-scene technique of stage and screen

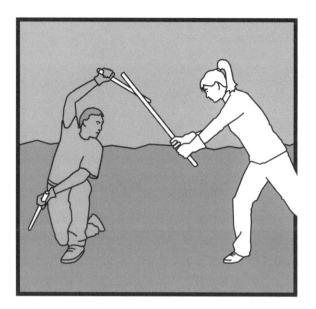

BUMPS AND BRUISES

DISTRUST

CUTS AND SCRAPES

REQUIRES

☐ 2 Cardboard Tubes
☐ Baggy Sweatshirts
☐ Gloves (optional)
☐ Friend

DURATION

DIFFICULTY

WARNING

Contrary to how it may appear, the person who hits is responsible for the safety of the person being hit. Do not hit your opponent's face and do not hit any harder than you would mind being hit yourself.

Supplementary Data

Fencing is rarely shown in movies because the blades (or "foils," as they are called) move too fast for the audience to follow. In fencing tournaments, contestants wear protective, electrically conductive armor that completes a circuit when it is touched by the opponent's foil. A computer is used to keep track of who touched who first because it is impossible for judges to see.

HOW-TO

Dramatic sword fighting is the kind of sword fighting that you see in movies and plays. The secret of dramatic sword fighting is this: always hit the other person's sword. Done properly, it will look like a very impressive battle!

1. **Prepare.** Put on baggy sweatshirts. The loose clothing will soften the blow of any accidental hits. Each of you pick up a cardboard tube and practice swinging it around so that you have a feel for how heavy and long it is. Stand facing each other, so that your swords hit mid-blade. This is your basic fighting distance.

2. **Decide** who will attack first.

3. **Simulate a hit.** The defender raises their sword in a defensive block. The attacker swings to hit that sword somewhere near the middle. It is up to the defender to decide where the attacker will attack. It is up to the attacker to hit the "target" (the middle of the sword).

4. **Switch roles.** The defender now becomes the attacker, and the attacker becomes the defender.

5. **Repeat** steps 3 and 4 until the transition between hits is fast and smooth. Increase the tempo as you get better. Any time either of the players is hit on the body instead of the sword, stop and figure out how it happened.

Once you can reliably trade hits quickly, you can start to move around. In movies they always go up and down stairs, and over furniture. After you get good at moving the battle around the environment, try adding dramatic dialog such as "Have at you!" and "Taste the bitter edge of my steel, scoundrel!" or "Hah! Your fancy swordplay will only delay your demise!" or even "Your powers are weak, old man."

For dramatic variation, you can vary the rhythm by having the attacker take two or three hits before becoming the defender. This makes it look like one person has the upper hand. To make it work in front of an audience, decide on a code word that lets the attacker know to take the extra hits.

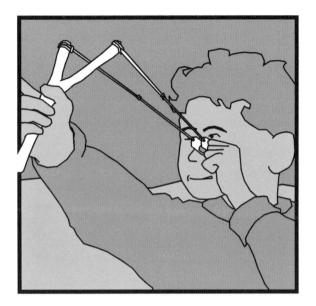

DANGER TO OTHERS

PROJECTILES

PROPERTY DAMAGE

REQUIRES

☐ Forked Stick
☐ Rubber Bands (medium-sized)
☐ Scrap of Leather or Cloth
☐ Pebbles, Peas, or Flower Buds
☐ Clear Area (without people, pets or things that might get damaged)

DURATION

DIFFICULTY

WARNING

Slingshots aren't inherently very dangerous, but releasing projectiles can be. Always know where you are pointing your slingshot and NEVER aim in the direction of a person or pet. You are responsible for every projectile you release.

HOW-TO

1. Make elastic bands. To begin, you can just tie two pairs of rubber bands together to make two long bands. If you find you want more power later, you can double up the rubber bands.

2. Make a pocket. Cut a small rectangle out of leather or a scrap of sturdy cloth. You can either tie the rubber bands to the pocket, or cut two small holes and loop the bands through.

3. Assemble. Tie the rubber bands to the ends of a forked stick. If the bands slip off, try lashing them in place with a bit of string.

4. Aim. Place a pebble in the pocket and trap it by pinching the pocket with thumb and forefinger. Hold the handle steady at arms length. Keep a light, but firm, grip on the pocket and pull back.

5. Fire. Release the pocket!

Slingshot masters say that the key to aiming is to hold the pocket steady and move the forked stick around to line up your shot. Aluminum cans make good targets: set 'em up and knock 'em down.

Accuracy comes from repetition. Gather together a pile of pebbles and spend a few minutes every day, aiming at a variety of targets. A slingshot master can hit a soda can from 20 paces.

Supplementary Data

The slingshot is a fairly modern invention, as these things go. It requires long, thin strips of stretchy rubber - a material produced first in the late 1800s and not widely available until early 1900s. The idea is really an update of the ancient sling (a leather pocket tied to two leather strips), the weapon purportedly used by David to bring down Goliath.

Rubber got its name from Joseph Priestley (inventor of soda water) who noticed that blobs of it were good for rubbing pencil marks off of paper.

If there were no air resistance to contend with, a pebble fired from a slingshot would travel in what is referred to as a ballistic trajectory. From the moment the pebble leaves the pocket of the slingshot, gravity bends its path down towards Earth. This prevents the pebble from orbiting the planet. Put the air back into the equation and the path gets even shorter. Without air resistance, your pebble would travel almost twice as far.

PROGRESS

Date: ___ / ___ / ___   I did it! ☐

www.fiftydangerousthings.com/topic/27

28 Climb a Tree
Take advantage of your opposable thumbs

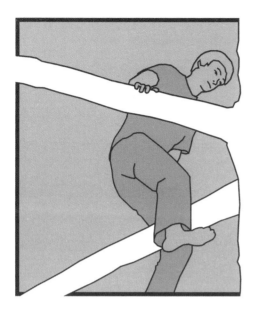

CUTS AND SCRAPES

FALL

BUMPS AND BRUISES

REQUIRES

☐ Good Shoes or Bare Feet
☐ Tree

DURATION

DIFFICULTY

WARNING

Falling out of a tree can result in serious injury, even death. However, it doesn't have to end that way: take your time and stay focused on the task at hand.

Supplementary Data

The concentric rings seen in the trunk of a tree are a cross-section of the nested cones that make up the structure. If you count the rings at the bottom of the tree you can determine the total age of the tree. If you were to cut off the top of a tree, you could see how long it took for just that chunk of the tree to grow.

Snow and rain can add a lot of extra weight to a branch and healthy branches can usually handle the load, but unless you have x-ray vision, it's best to do your tree-climbing in dry weather.

HOW-TO

There are a few simple rules to follow when ascending a tree:

• Stay close to the trunk - climbing out on a branch increases the chance that the branch will break.

• Never reach up higher than your chest - you're going to have to climb back down so don't make problems for yourself later by reaching up too high for the next branch.

• Never trust a dead branch - you just can't tell how much weight it will hold and for how long. If you can't see any leaves on it, don't trust it.

• Stay focused - pay attention to what you are doing. Look at each place you grab, every place you step, and don't yell "Look at me!" You're climbing - this is serious work.

You can't always find a tree to climb when you need one, so keep an eye out for a tree that you like and make a plan to go back and climb it when you have time. A perfect climbing tree has branches that are leafy on the ends, evenly spaced, and easy to reach.

1. Climb up. There may be multiple paths up a tree - take a moment to make a plan of attack and then start climbing.

2. Enjoy the view. Find a nice branch to stop at. Sit with your back partly against the tree so that you don't accidentally tip over and enjoy your arboreal perch.

3. Climb down. Getting back down is a little harder than climbing up because you can't always see where your feet are going. Take your time, stay close to the trunk, and step so that the branch is centered under the arch of your foot.

Start out by only climbing up a few branches and coming back down before you decide to go really high. You'll want to be as comfortable climbing down as you are climbing up so that you don't get stuck.

PROGRESS

Date: ___ / ___ / ___   I did it! ☐

www.fiftydangerousthings.com/topic/28

EMBARRASS-MENT

GET A TICKET

REQUIRES

- ☐ Courage
- ☐ Sign
- ☐ Hat (or other container)
- ☐ Props (optional)

DURATION   **DIFFICULTY**

WARNING

Check local street signs for regulations. Some areas have strict rules about where, and during what hours, people may perform on the street.

Supplementary Data

Some of the most well-known musicians and artists started out busking: The Blue Man Group, Russell Crowe, Dixie Chicks, Pierce Brosnan, Bob Dylan, Taylor Swift, KT Tunstall, Penn and Teller, and thousands of other famous people you have heard of.

Pickpockets are thieves who are adept at stealing people's wallets without them noticing. It is common for pickpockets to work in crowds that gather around buskers because everyone's attention is on the busker and they are less likely to feel their wallet being taken.

HOW-TO

Entertaining people on the street, to try and get them to give you money, is called "busking." You don't have to be able to sing or play music - buskers also make drawings, tell jokes and stories, compliment people's outfits, juggle, perform tricks - almost anything you know how to do that can be done outside will work.

1. Design your act. Decide what you are going to do and practice it in front of a mirror. Do you want to wear a costume? Do you need other props? Work it all out before you get to the street.

2. Advertise. Make a sign that clearly states what you do. It could be as simple as "Compliments given, donations appreciated" or "Draw your picture in 5 seconds, 10 cents."

3. Choose your spot. Look for a sidewalk with some space and good pedestrian traffic. If other people are already there busking, that's an indication that you thought of a good spot - but you will need to find your own spot.

4. Put out a hat and sign. An upside-down hat is a signal to people that you accept donations, although a can works, too.

5. Do your thing!

The tradition of busking extends back through recorded history, and throughout that time there have always been hecklers - people who make fun of performers. Buskers generally agree that the best way to deal with hecklers is to have a witty comeback. For example, if a heckler yells "You stink!," you could reply with something like "Perhaps, but at least my mother stopped picking out my clothes years ago," or "I don't know what your problem is... but I bet it's hard to pronounce," or "Thanks! I started with nothing and I've still got most of it left."

PROGRESS

Date: ___ / ___ / ___   I did it! ☐

www.fiftydangerousthings.com/topic/29

30 | Dam up a Creek
Change the course of history (momentarily)

EROSION

PARASITES

REQUIRES

☐ Creek

DURATION

DIFFICULTY

WARNING

Due to human agriculture and livestock, virtually all watersheds in the United States and Europe are contaminated with water-borne parasites. Unless explicitly told otherwise, do not drink the water in any creek.

Supplementary Data

The Colorado River has seven significant dams restricting and managing its natural flow. So much of the river is diverted to aqueducts that it no longer reaches the Sea of Cortez in Mexico.

The Hoover Dam was the first arch-gravity dam ever built at that scale. The arched shape of the concrete barrier distributes the weight of the water into the canyon walls instead of just resisting through sheer weight alone.

Besides reducing the flow of water in a river, a dam changes the temperature of the water downstream.

HOW-TO

1. Find a suitable creek. Look for water running in a channel that is less than a foot wide. In order to ensure that you don't destroy any significant natural features, look for sections that will be flushed in the next big rain.

2. Pick your spot. Think of the Hoover Dam: a tall concrete wall in a narrow canyon. You want a place where the creek is narrow, but not flowing so swiftly that it will wash away your dam while you are building it.

3. Gather materials to build with. You can use almost anything: leaves, sticks, mud, rocks, sand, gravel. Be sure you only use material that you find in or alongside the creek. The material you find will determine how you construct your dam.

4. Build your dam. If the water backing up is causing trouble, consider a temporary re-routing of the creek somewhere upstream. This is a common step in the construction of large dams. As the reservoir behind your dam fills, the pressure on the base of the dam will increase. This pressure can undermine your dam, causing it to leak or catastrophically blow out. Rocks placed at the base on the dry side of your dam can help prevent that.

5. Deconstruct your dam. Even with a multi-day project, it's important to restore the creek to its original condition when you are done.

By building a dam, you are changing fast running water into standing water. This might be a good thing if you are trying to make a pond for frogs, but you are also making a breeding ground for mosquitoes.

It is possible that your little dam could lead to a major shift in the course of the creek over time, even after you have removed it. This is a responsibility that you must consider when choosing where to build a dam.

PROGRESS

Date: ___ / ___ / ___   I did it! ☐

www.fiftydangerousthings.com/topic/30

CLAUSTRO-PHOBIA

VERMIN

CLONKED

REQUIRES

☐ Flashlight or Headlamp
☐ Rope
☐ Boots
☐ Gloves
☐ Helmet
☐ Adult

DURATION **DIFFICULTY**

WARNING

Climbing around in a culvert or other man-made tunnel may expose you to rusty or sharp metal - wear gloves and a helmet at all times. Observe all posted warnings and restrictions. Do not go further than the end of your rope and never lose sight of the entrance.

HOW-TO

1. Find a good hole. Look for places where a creek goes under a road, or find a storm drain (to be entered only during dry weather) of sufficient size.

2. Assess the risks. How recently was this hole built? Is the metal rusty, is the concrete crumbling? What kind of water, if any, flows through it? Avoid anything that carries sewage, shows signs of rats or other vermin, or is populated by unsavory characters.

3. Prepare. Put on gloves, helmet, and boots.

4. Anchor. Tie one end of the rope around your waist and give the other end to the adult.

5. Explore. Enter the cave, culvert, or storm drain. Pay careful attention to the surfaces you are touching - things can get slimy and slippery underground.

When you are underground, take a moment to close your eyes and listen. Sounds from far away can be carried through connecting tunnels in surprising ways. Can you identify the sources of all of the sounds you hear? If you were a gopher, you could sense the vibrations of a predator walking above ground.

Supplementary Data

The oldest cave paintings yet discovered are in the Chauvet cave in France. Archeologists, using carbon-dating techniques, estimate the images of horses, lions and other animals were painted 32,000 years ago.

Claustrophobia is how psychiatrists describe an irrational fear of confined spaces. People sometimes develop claustrophobia when they get stuck in elevators for a little while.

Humans did not evolve for life underground, but we have, as a species, always taken advantage of the natural shelter and defensibility of caves. Cave-dwelling creatures have evolved heightened senses of hearing and touch that enable them to survive in a world without light. When we visit the underground, we soon discover the limits of our surface-adapted senses.

Big, old cities like Paris and London often have vast networks of abandoned tunnels and passageways underneath them. Most of them are unsafe to enter or explore without special equipment and planning.

PROGRESS

Date: ___ / ___ / ___   I did it! ☐

www.fiftydangerousthings.com/topic/31

CUTS AND SCRAPES

CRUSHED

BUMPS AND BRUISES

REQUIRES

☐ Car (and owner's manual)
☐ Jack
☐ Tire Iron
☐ Wheel Blocks
☐ Adult (tires are REALLY heavy)

DURATION   **DIFFICULTY**

WARNING

A car that is up on a jack should never be considered stable, even with all the tires blocked. Don't put any part of your body under, or attempt to get into, the car. Wheel nuts (also called "lug nuts") must be tightened by a person weighing more than 100 lbs. Tires, although filled with air, are still really heavy - get help lifting the tire.

Supplementary Data

Tires are manufactured at a global rate of about one billion per year.

The alphanumerical gibberish embossed on the side of a tire encodes an astonishing amount of information. For example, the first letters specify the vehicle type: P for passenger vehicle, LT for light truck, ST for special trailer, and T for temporary spare tire.

HOW-TO

Since you probably don't need to swap the tire on the car for a new one right now, you can practice by unmounting and remounting the same tire.

1. Read the owner's manual. It will have a section dedicated to the topic of changing a tire. Pay special attention to the details regarding proper placement of the jack.

2. Prepare. Find a place to park the car where you won't be sitting in the street while you change the tire. Place blocks to prevent the car from rolling when it gets lifted by the jack. If there is any slope where you are changing the tire, put the blocks on the downhill side of each tire. If it is perfectly flat, then put the blocks in front of the front tires and behind the back tires.

3. Remove the tire. Following the directions in the owner's manual, lift the car using the jack and remove the tire. In general this will mean positioning the jack, loosening the lug nuts, raising the car, removing the lug nuts, and unmounting the tire.

4. Move the tire. Roll the tire around a bit to get a feel for what it is like to move. If you actually had a flat tire, you would have to swap it with the spare in the trunk.

5. Remount the tire. Again following the owner's manual, put the tire back on the car. This will mean aligning the tire with the lugs, putting it up on the wheel, finger-tightening the lug nuts, lowering the car, and tightening the lug nuts the rest of the way.

6. Verify. Have the owner of the car double-check the mounted tire, and the tightness of the lug nuts.

A car is merely a collection of parts assembled in a particular way. Like any manufactured item, it can be taken apart and put back together.

PROGRESS

Date: ___ / ___ / ___   I did it! ☐

www.fiftydangerousthings.com/topic/32

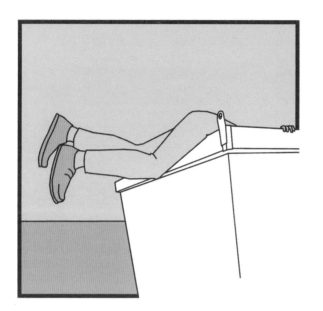

BIOHAZARD

GET A TICKET

CUTS AND SCRAPES

REQUIRES

☐ Dumpster (or trash bin)
☐ Gloves
☐ Long Sleeved Shirt
☐ Long Pants
☐ Sturdy Shoes
☐ Adult Supervision

DURATION

DIFFICULTY

WARNING

A dumpster can be a dangerous place. The people who throw things into dumpsters aren't thinking that someone might climb in there, so they throw away broken glass, weird chemicals, and coffee grounds. Avoid dumpsters that may contain biohazards such as medical waste or diapers. Always look carefully before climbing in, and move carefully while you are in there.

```
Supplementary Data

You can tell a lot about what a company
is making, or doing, based on what
you find in their dumpsters. Sometimes
a company will try to get a peek in
the dumpsters of a competing company
to see what they are working on. This
is called industrial espionage, and
according to current business reports
it happens all the time.
```

If you find a dumpster with something interesting in it, remember where you found it and check back occasionally. If that interesting stuff keeps showing up, you may be able to talk to the person or business that is putting it in the dumpster and get them to set it aside for you to pick up later.

An alternative source for rescuing interesting items is "bulk trash" day. Some areas have a special day for all the items that don't fit in the regular garbage can.

HOW-TO

Most dumpsters are yucky and dangerous, but there are good dumpsters out there, full of interesting stuff. If you are persistent, and you take a peek in the occasional dumpster now and then, you will learn which ones are good and which ones to avoid.

1. Find a dumpster. The best dumpsters are often in the industrial part of town. Dumpsters behind restaurants tend to be the dirtiest. Dumpsters behind manufacturing facilities are often interesting. Avoid any dumpsters near hospitals, medical clinics, or apartment buildings.

2. Have a look. Put on gloves and open the lid all the way. You don't want the lid to bang you on the head, possibly knocking you out, or trapping you in the dumpster. Look carefully at what you can see. Are there any visible dangers? If there are, you have three options: find another dumpster, move or cover the dangerous item, or just completely avoid that part of the dumpster.

3. Climb in. Dumpsters are not designed to climb in and out of, so take your time and have a plan for getting back out.

4. Look for good stuff. Are there good project materials around? Interesting things that could be taken apart?

5. Hand the good stuff out to your assistant.

PROGRESS

Date: ___ / ___ / ___   I did it! ☐

www.fiftydangerousthings.com/topic/33

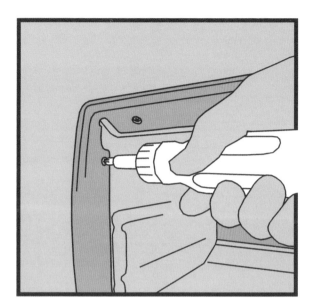

CUTS AND SCRAPES

PROJECTILES

MAKE A MESS

REQUIRES

- ☐ Broken Appliance
- ☐ Screwdriver
- ☐ Pliers
- ☐ Crescent Wrench
- ☐ Wire Cutters
- ☐ Safety Goggles
- ☐ Cardboard or Drop Cloth

DURATION   **DIFFICULTY**

WARNING

There are a few appliances that should not be taken apart without expert guidance: old tube televisions, CRT monitors, and refrigerators, to name a few. Read and understand any labels and safety warnings you can find on the appliance before opening it. Wear safety goggles and watch out for mechanisms that may contain compressed springs such as self-closing doors and trays. If you're not sure it's safe to open, do some research.

HOW-TO

Taking things apart is more of a process than a sequence of steps. Remember, it's only deconstruction if you don't break anything, otherwise it's just destruction.

1. Prepare to operate. Find a place to work where you won't lose parts that come loose. Cover the work surface with cardboard or a drop cloth so that you don't have to worry about accidentally making scratches.

2. Analyze. Make a complete examination of the exterior of the appliance. Look under labels for hidden screws, disguised tabs, and connectors, and make a plan of attack.

3. Deconstruct. Remove screws, connectors, and parts that are easy first. As you remove parts, try to figure out what they are for.

4. Reconnoiter. If you get stuck, try to figure out how the part that is blocking your progress was put together; if you can figure out how it was assembled, you can usually figure out how to get it apart. If all else fails, try to figure out how to do the least damage necessary to keep making progress.

5. Persist. Repeat steps 3 and 4 until there is nothing left to take apart.

Manufacturers sometimes use glue as a fastener. This makes deconstruction (and repair) difficult, if not impossible. A little gentle

---

Supplementary Data

Press-fit is a technique, used in the manufacture of many home electronics, where tabs and shafts are forced into slots and holes that are a little too small by very powerful hydraulic presses. These connections are notoriously difficult to loosen and often must be bent, snapped, or cut to remove.

---

prying can sometimes break the glue without breaking the parts, but care must be taken.

Over time, as you take more things apart, you will start to collect odd bits and pieces. A few jars with lids, or other food storage containers, are convenient for keeping small screws, gears, and springs.

Now, what will you make with all those parts?

PROGRESS

Date: ___ / ___ / ___   I did it! ☐

www.fiftydangerousthings.com/topic/34

BAD STINK

VERMIN

REQUIRES

- ☐ Car
- ☐ Sturdy Shoes
- ☐ Money (maybe)
- ☐ Adult

DURATION

DIFFICULTY

WARNING

There are significant hazards at the dump, but a little common sense will keep you safe. Every dump is different and the regulations that they operate under will vary by location, so it's best to obey the posted warnings and signs.

HOW-TO

1. Locate your regional landfill. Garbage processing facilities come in two basic varieties: transfer stations and landfills. The transfer station is just a stop-over on the way to the landfill. Garbage trucks usually take garbage to transfer stations, but people who work with garbage usually know where it goes after the transfer station.

2. Drive to the landfill. There is little chance that public transit can get you there, and they are not likely to let you walk in, so it's best to get an adult to take you. Bring a few bags of garbage with you.

3. Pay the entrance fee. The landfill often charges people to dump garbage, so you may have to pay a small fee to enter.

4. Explore. There are probably separate areas for recycling cans, glass, metal and batteries, and disposing of paints, toxic chemicals, appliances and wrecked vehicles. Everything else goes into the ground where giant machines compress it and cover it with dirt.

5. Pay attention, take pictures. This is the end of the line for everything we make and buy.

Like most places, if you show an interest in what they are doing and ask intelligent questions, the people who work at the landfill may be willing to give you a guided tour or at the very least point out things that you might not otherwise notice.

```
Supplementary Data

On average, Americans generate more
than four pounds of trash per person
per day - almost twice the average
amount generated per person in other
major countries. This amounts to 146
million tons of unrecycled material
every year, which is enough to fill
55,000 football fields to a depth of
six feet.

A dump is a big hole in the ground that
people just pile garbage in; a land-
fill is a system for isolating trash
from the environment. Landfills can be
below ground with either a plastic
or clay liner, or above ground with
a protective layer underneath them.

Search for "Mount Trashmore" on the
internet and you will discover that
there are dozens of man-made moun-
tains in the United States. These are
above-ground landfills that have been
covered with soil and planted with
grasses and trees to make a park.
```

If your landfill is located a long way from your transfer station (such as in New York City), the transfer station is likely big enough to be an interesting destination.

PROGRESS

Date: ___ / ___ / ___   I did it! ☐

www.fiftydangerousthings.com/topic/35

BURNS

UPSET STOMACH

DISTRUST

REQUIRES

- ☐ Cookie Ingredients and Recipe
- ☐ Oven
- ☐ Oven Mitts or Pot Holders
- ☐ Salt
- ☐ Cookie Sheet
- ☐ Extra Mixing Bowls
- ☐ Friend

DURATION

DIFFICULTY

WARNING

Things that have been in the oven can be very hot. Use a pot holder or oven mitt to safely handle the cookies and cookie sheet.

HOW-TO

1. Make a batch of your favorite cookie batter by following the recipe.

2. When you are at the stage where you have liquid ingredients and dry ingredients - but you have not mixed them together - split them into two equal portions. Now you should have two sets of dry ingredients and two sets of liquid ingredients.

3. In one set of dry ingredients, add 3 to 4 tablespoons of salt and mix well.

4. Combine wet and dry ingredients as described in the recipe to make two batches of batter - keep track of which one is salty if you want to avoid eating the "poisoned" cookies.

5. Bake as directed.

You are now ready to "poison" your friends! Tricking your friends into biting into a salty cookie might be easy the first time; getting them to do it the second time may take some planning.

But, remember this: every time you trick your friend, they will trust you a little bit less. It may take more than a good cookie to regain their good favor.

Are you brave enough to taste one of your own "poisoned" cookies?

Supplementary Data

A "con" is a trick that criminals do to get money from strangers; a person who is very good at it is called a "con artist." The term was created by shortening the word confidence. There are hundreds of cons, and they all have strange names.

A famous con is called "the pig in a poke." A "poke" is another name for a sack. This trick was played on farmers starting at least 500 years ago! A con artist holds open a bag and shows the farmer a live healthy piglet and states a price. The farmer hands over his money, but when the con artist turns away to get the farmer's change, he switches the sack for one containing a cat. He then hands the bag with the cat to the farmer with his change. This con is why people sometimes say "don't buy a pig in a poke" - meaning you shouldn't buy something without seeing it first. This is also why people say "let the cat out of the bag" - meaning to reveal a trick or secret.

PROGRESS

Date: ___ / ___ / ___   I did it! ☐

www.fiftydangerousthings.com/topic/36

TRIP

COLD

ELECTRO-CUTION

REQUIRES

- ☐ Wind Storm
- ☐ Kite String
- ☐ Newspaper, Sticks, Tape, Scissors
- ☐ Gloves
- ☐ Friend

DURATION

DIFFICULTY

WARNING

Do not fly your kite when there is a chance of lightning. It is easy to lose track of where you are when you are running while looking up at a kite. Make sure your kiting area is free of obstacles like park benches, fallen logs, or holes that you might step in.

Supplementary Data

The bridle sets what aeronautical engineers call "the angle of attack." They use this term to describe how a wing meets the wind. In high winds, tuning the angle of attack is very important.

The friction from air blowing over the surface of the kite and along the tail creates "drag." It is the drag on the tail that keeps the kite pointed up.

HOW-TO

Howling winds present a unique opportunity for a different kind of kite flying. Rather than work to keep your kite aloft, your goal will be to see how long your kite lasts.

1. Build a kite. Given enough wind, anything can fly. Now that you have enough wind, you can experiment with kite design. The goal here is not to make the perfect kite, but to make something that can both fly and withstand the force of the wind. Make something quick and simple so that you can test and refine it easily.

2. Attach a bridle and tail. If the bridle loop is too close to the nose of the kite (the angle of attack is low), the kite will nose-dive. If the loop is too far back (the angle of attack is high), the kite will not climb away from the ground. If the kite spins too much, try adding another length of tail. If the tail is too heavy it will prevent the kite from flying.

3. Attach a string. Instead of using the whole spool, measure and cut a piece about 50 feet long. Tie a stick to the loose end to make it easy to hold when the kite is flying. With string attached, you are now ready to fly.

4. Launch. Stand with your back to the wind and get a firm grip on the string. Hand the kite to your friend and take ten steps backward, paying out string as you go. Gently tug the string as your friend releases the kite.

Kites don't always fly at first and yours will likely need some adjustments before it behaves in a strong wind. Play with the bridle and the length of the tail and you will find the right combination for the weather conditions. If the kite breaks, figure out why and head back inside to refine and rebuild.

Strong winds can be turbulent; for consistent wind you may need to find an open field without many trees.

With some tuning and a little practice the kite should rise up and tug at the string like a wild animal. How else is it different than in light wind?

PROGRESS

Date: ___ / ___ / ___   I did it! ☐

www.fiftydangerousthings.com/topic/37

FRUSTRATION

FALL

**SPRAINED
ANKLE**

REQUIRES

☐ Sidewalk
☐ Railroad Track, Parking Curb (or similar)

DURATION   **DIFFICULTY**

WARNING

Never walk on anything that you wouldn't mind falling from. Before trying anything tall, you might want to master #16 Drop from High Places.

Supplementary Data

The technical term for tightrope walking is "funambulism," from the Latin "funis" meaning rope, and "ambulare" meaning walk. Somnambulism is sleep walking. Lunambulists are people who sleepwalk in the moonlight (although the word looks more like it should mean moon-walking).

You stay balanced when you are standing up through a combination of information from your eyes, your vestibular system (organs in your inner ear), and proprioception (information from your muscles and joints). Sighted people rely more heavily on their vision, which is why they have trouble balancing when they close their eyes.

You are an upside-down pendulum; holding your arms out spreads out your center of mass, reducing your angular velocity, which gives you more time to make balance corrections.

Philippe Petit and a crew of helpers snuck onto the rooftops of the Twin Towers on August 7th, 1974 and constructed a tightrope between the two buildings. Philippe then spent 45 minutes walking back and forth, lying down, and even dancing on the rope, 1368 feet above the streets below.

HOW-TO

You can learn to walk a tightrope by first developing your sense of balance on everyday objects like rails and fences.

1. Trust your balance. Find a place on a sidewalk with a long straight crack. Pretend the crack is a tightrope and walk back and forth along it. Keep your eyes up, looking at the horizon. Use your peripheral vision to follow the crack and keep your feet on it. Notice how you do not lose your balance once you walk naturally.

2. Use your balance. Find an abandoned, or seldom used, railroad track. A parking curb, low wall, fence, or horizontal pipe will work too. Just be sure there are no obstacles or traffic nearby. Pretend the rail is the crack from step 1, and walk back and forth along it.

3. Keep your eyes up. Looking at the horizon will make it easier to balance. Feel the rail with your feet and use your peripheral vision to follow the rail.

When you lose your balance, it is better to step off and back on the rail than to flail your arms. We don't normally walk around staring down at our feet, which is why when we are trying to walk on a rail, staring down at the rail makes it harder to stay balanced.

The secret of tightrope walking is to understand that the rope is just like the crack in the sidewalk.

PROGRESS

Date: ___ / ___ / ___   I did it! ☐

www.fiftydangerousthings.com/topic/38

Cook Something in the Dishwasher
Discover the hidden potential in common machines

FOOD POISONING

☐ Aluminum Foil
☐ Raw Chicken, Hot Dogs or Vegetables
☐ Butter
☐ Salt or Spices (optional)
☐ Meat Thermometer (or Adult)

DURATION

DIFFICULTY

WARNING

Undercooked chicken can be unsafe to eat. Check your food carefully before consuming. Use a meat thermometer or ask an adult.

Supplementary Data

Dishwashers don't actually scrub dishes - they just squirt water relentlessly around the dish compartment until everything gets clean. This process is aided by powerful cleaning agents in dishwashing soaps, including various phosphate compounds added to prevent calcium and magnesium (found in most tap water) from clouding up glassware. The phosphates are responsible for some giant algae blooms in bodies of water near cities.

While it is still possible to wash dishes as efficiently as a modern dishwasher, most people use more than twice as much water to hand-wash a full load of dishes.

HOW-TO

Cooking in the dishwasher is not much different than baking, you just need to keep the food from getting soapy.

1. Prepare food. Cut chicken into strips about ½ inch wide. If you don't like chicken, hot dogs, vegetables, or apples work just as well. Place food in center of a sheet of foil. Dab with butter and add salt or spices if you like.

2. Seal it up. Fold up, then carefully roll the edges of the foil to create a watertight packet. You can add another layer of foil if your foil is thin. Place packet in top rack of dishwasher (middle if you have three racks) and finish loading the dishwasher with dirty dishes. Do not let packet get punctured by the rack or any dishes.

3. Cook it. Run the dishwasher on the hottest setting (at or above 160°F). After the wash cycle finishes, make sure the dry cycle completes before opening.

4. Check it. Carefully remove the foil packet from the dishwasher and examine for punctures. Discard and try again with the next load of dishes if any holes are found. Open the packet and check to make sure your chicken is thoroughly cooked.

5. Enjoy. Toast goes particularly well with dishwasher chicken.

An oven is an insulated box with a heating element inside. Looked at that way, is the dishwasher that much different? Sure it has spray arms for water and uses soap, but it is also insulated and has a heating element. That makes it an oven - with a few extra features thrown in.

Now, if only there was a way to make toast without using the toaster....

BEE STING

FRUSTRATION

WARNING

Bee stings can be very painful. If you find a hive, do not approach it without some protective clothing. Some people are severely allergic to bee stings; if you are one of those people you might skip this activity.

Supplementary Data

Bees, ants, and termites are evolved from wasps. Wasps and honey bees look similar, but the honey bees are hairy and wasps are not. Bumblebees are also hairy, but have much rounder, larger bodies than honey bees.

Honey bees can only sting once, leaving their stinger behind and dying as a result. Wasps and bumblebees can sting multiple times.

Wasps, and the insects that evolved from them, are considered "social," and as such are nearly unique in the animal kingdom. In social insect nests, there is a "queen" responsible for laying all of the eggs, and multitudes of "workers" who maintain the colony. The workers will readily sacrifice themselves to save the nest should the need arise.

HOW-TO

There is no perfect recipe for finding a hive - it is a process of careful observation and detective work. Start by locating flowers or plants that attract bees. Bees are adventurous explorers and may travel as far as a mile and a half away from their nest to collect pollen and nectar. In cities they will visit window boxes and backyard gardens, and in the country they can be found in any field or in the weeds and flowers that grow along roadsides.

Once you have found where the bees are foraging, you must try to figure out where they go when they are fully laden. A heavily laden bee is slower than a bee fresh from the nest, so they are easier to follow. Even so, it is very hard to keep your eye on a single bee for any length of time so this is most easily done in the late afternoon when they are all returning to the colony at once.

Depending on how much time you have on a given day, you may have to do your hunt for the hive in stages. First, determine what direction the bees are generally heading when leaving the area and follow them as far as you can. Remember that spot and you can return there to watch for more bees to pass by and pick up the chase. Keep repeating the process and you can make your way back to the colony.

Depending on what type of colony you find, there may be as few as ten bees or as many as thousands, if it is a man-made hive with a healthy population. In either case it's important not to disturb the nest. An angry colony can deliver a lot of stings in a short amount of time.

Bees sometimes make their nests high up in trees or buildings. You may have to track a few colonies before you find one that is visible from ground level.

PROGRESS

Date: ___ / ___ / ___   I did it! ☐

www.fiftydangerousthings.com/topic/40

WANDERLUST

IN-CONVENIENCE

TRAFFIC

REQUIRES

- ☐ Bus/Train Fare
- ☐ Cellphone
- ☐ Transit Map

DURATION

DIFFICULTY

WARNING

Observe all posted safety warnings in stations and on buses and trains. Be careful in crowds; packs of adults move quickly during commute hours and do not always notice kids.

Supplementary Data

You are approximately ten times safer traveling by public transit than by private automobile.

With 140,700 miles of track, the United States has the largest railway system in the world, yet it moves fewer people by rail than India, which has one-fourth as much track.

Transit systems are measured in "passenger miles per gallon." Suppose a car gets 30 mpg. If one person drives the car, then that's 30 passenger miles per gallon. If someone rides with them, then it's 60 passenger miles per gallon. A bus with no riders gets 6 passenger miles per gallon, but filled up with 40 riders it gets 240 passenger miles per gallon, which is 8 times more efficient than the car with just one driver.

HOW-TO

If you can find your way somewhere that means you can find your way home, too, should the need ever arise.

1. Pick a destination. For this project, the place you go is not as important as the journey.

2. Plan your route and write it down. Starting from the bus or train stop nearest your house, figure out which transit lines you will use and where you will have to change buses or trains. There are always trade-offs when using public transit.

3. Carry cash, but not too much. Be prepared to pay for fares plus a little extra in case you have to change your route. Keep your money securely stashed, perhaps in a front pocket. Don't forget to make sure your cellphone is fully charged.

4. Catch the bus (or train). Walk from your home to the bus stop or train station nearest you and start your journey.

5. Observe. Pay attention to your surroundings and notice what you can see from this new perspective. Traveling on your own is liberating, but you are responsible for your trip.

6. Check in. Call home using the cellphone when you reach your destination. How you get back home should be obvious.

Things do not always go as planned: buses break down, trains are delayed, traffic grinds to a halt, schedules are changed. It's good to know how to read a transit map so you can adapt your plan on the fly. If lost or confused, drivers and ticket booth operators will have more reliable information than other passengers.

If that project proved too easy for you, try it again, but this time skip the planning step and figure out how to get where you are going using transit system maps while en route.

Field Notes
Observations, improvements, new ideas

41

PROGRESS

Date: ___ / ___ / ___   I did it! ☐

www.fiftydangerousthings.com/topic/41

BAD STINK

UPSET STOMACH

SMOKE DETECTOR

REQUIRES

- [ ] Oven
- [ ] Oven Mitts or Pot Holders
- [ ] Baking Ingredients (at least flour, butter, eggs/milk)
- [ ] Mixing Bowl
- [ ] Cake or Muffin Pan
- [ ] Paper Towel

DURATION | DIFFICULTY

WARNING

While we encourage you to be experimental, do not be tempted to include any non-food ingredients in your recipe. Things that have been in the oven can be very hot. Use a pot holder or oven mitt to safely handle the pan.

```
Supplementary Data

Baking soda releases carbon dioxide
gas when it reacts with acids, so
bakers often add it to recipes to
make things fluffy. The reaction is
endothermic, meaning that it needs
heat energy to happen - which is good
because you don't want all of the gas
to come out in the mixing bowl, you
want it to wait until it gets in the
oven.
```

HOW-TO

Inventing something new is a process of experimenting, testing, and refining. There are a nearly infinite number of possible desserts, but to explore new territory you will have to try some radical combinations - which means you may make a few horrible concoctions before you discover something new and delicious.

1. Collect ingredients. Pull out the things that you know you like and arrange them on the counter. Try pairing up items that you think might go well together. Now is a good time to preheat the oven. 350°F is a good temperature to try baking a new recipe.

2. Make a dough. The dough is what holds everything together. Flour, milk and eggs are usually the key ingredients, but there are other solutions as well (custards just use eggs and milk).

3. Get creative. Mix in the ingredients you've selected, such as spices, raisins, chocolate chips, potato chips, or ???. Once it's ready to go in the oven, write your recipe down.

4. Prepare a pan. Grease the pan by smearing butter on the interior surfaces with a paper towel, then lightly dust with flour. Tip the pan and tap the sides to spread it around, then turn the pan over the sink and tap it to remove any excess flour that doesn't adhere to the butter.

5. Pour your creation into the pan.

6. Cook until done. Check it visually every 5 to 10 minutes. When the top starts to brown, poke it with a clean butter knife. If the knife comes out clean, then the insides are cooked. Write down the total cooking time.

7. Turn off the oven. Remove the hot pan from the oven using oven mitts and set it aside to cool (if the stove is off, that's a good place to put it). Wait at least 10 minutes.

8. Enjoy. Write a summary of how it turned out and ideas for next time.

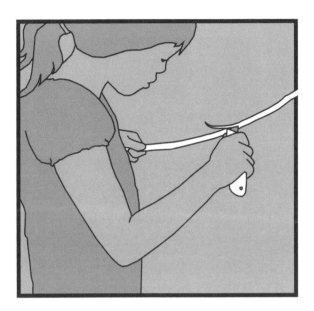

**CUTS AND
SCRAPES**

FRUSTRATION

**PROPERTY
DAMAGE**

REQUIRES

☐ Stick
☐ Pocket or Utility Knife
☐ Patience
☐ Adult Supervision

DURATION

DIFFICULTY

WARNING

Only use knives with locking blades. Never force the blade, and don't try to remove too much wood at a time. Work where there are no people in the zone of your knife and always cut away from your body.

Supplementary Data

Inuit children are trained by the age of four to use razor-sharp knives to cut the seal blubber that is a staple in their diets.

The same basic whittling technique described here has been used to carve things as small as a human hair and as big as a dugout canoe.

Before the age of metal, sharp rocks were used to carve wood. The oldest pocketknife ever found was made more than 2500 years ago.

HOW-TO

Once you can shape wood, you can make almost anything. But woodcarving is like learning to play guitar - it takes time and requires persistence. Don't expect it be easy the first time you try.

1. Practice opening and closing the knife safely and reliably. Open the knife and lock the blade. Hold the knife in your dominant hand (right if you are right-handed, left if you are left-handed) and hold a stick in your other hand.

2. Bring the blade and stick together so that the stick is touching the middle of the cutting edge of the blade. Angle the blade so that it will cut into the wood. You don't want it to just slide over the surface, but you are not trying to saw through the stick either. You might start out by just trying to shave the bark off the wood.

3. Apply pressure so that the cutting edge "bites" into the wood. The deeper the knife goes into the wood, the harder it is to cut. Try cutting shallower if you have trouble pushing the knife through the wood.

4. As the knife lifts a shaving of wood, flatten the blade against the stick and it will separate the shaving and come out of the wood as you push away.

Repeat steps 2 through 4 until you are able to easily shave wood off of the stick. Try making a section of the stick square by flattening each side.

Be patient, whittling is not about speed - it is about control.

Sometimes it is nice to just sit and whittle a stick. It's good practice and there is something satisfying about watching the wood as it curls off the knife.

Once you have mastered the basic skill of shaving wood off of a stick, there are hundreds of other techniques you can learn: notching, drilling, carving, and joining to name just a few.

Using a knife responsibly is the first step towards owning a pocketknife.

PROGRESS

Date: ___ / ___ / ___   I did it! ☐

www.fiftydangerousthings.com/topic/43

**CUTS AND
SCRAPES**

FALL

**BUMPS AND
BRUISES**

REQUIRES

- ☐ Strong Rope
- ☐ Sturdy Tree Branch
- ☐ Adult Supervision

DURATION   **DIFFICULTY**

WARNING

A healthy-looking branch can be rotten on the inside. Before you risk life and limb, inspect your hang-point carefully. Have an adult confirm your choice of branch. Pulling on it with a rope (while on solid ground) can provide good information.

Supplementary Data

A person on a swing is what physics textbooks call a pendulum. The rate at which a pendulum swings is determined by the length of the rope from the attachment point to the swinging mass (that's you). When we "pump" to make a swing go higher, we are really changing the length of the pendulum. We lay back (which lengthens the pendulum) as the swing goes down, and sit up (shortening the pendulum) as it goes up. It's the fast bit at the end of the arc that makes us go a little higher. This exchange of energy is called Conservation of Angular Momentum.

HOW-TO

1. Find a tree. Look for branches that are about as big around as your waist, have lots of green leaves at the ends, and no big rocks or roots directly below them. Sometimes ropes get stuck in trees - will you be able to get up to the branch to get your rope down later if needed?

2. Find suitable rope. Look for rope that can hold at least twice your weight (according to the "test weight" on the package). If you can't find rope that strong, then double- or triple-up the rope you have until it can hold twice your weight. You'll need it to be long enough to go up to your branch and back down, plus some extra for knots and loops.

3. Hang your rope. Holding on to the tail of the rope, throw the other end over the branch. If the branch is too high to do this easily, consider tying a rock to a length of string and tossing that over first, then use the string to pull the rope over.

4. Check the position. Make sure that your rope goes over the branch at the right spot. If it is too far from the tree, the branch may bend or break; too close and you may bump into the trunk when you are swinging.

5. Make fast. Repeat steps 3 and 4 again so that the rope wraps completely around the branch. This will keep it from slipping or sawing through the branch while you are swinging.

6. Swing!

You can just hang on to the rope to swing, but you may soon find that your desire to swing outlasts your ability to hold the rope. Tie a stopper-knot in the rope to make it easier to hang on to, or tie something on the very end to sit on, for example, a board or a tire.

If you are in a park, you probably shouldn't leave your swing tied to the tree. Untie any knots that you have tied, and then throw the rope back over the branch so that you can pull it down.

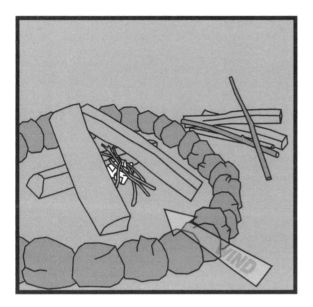

BURNS

FIRE

PROPERTY DAMAGE

REQUIRES

- ☐ Fire Pit, Ring, or Barbecue
- ☐ Water Bucket
- ☐ Firewood - various sized logs, or wood cut to various widths
- ☐ Kindling (twigs, small sticks or wood slivers)
- ☐ Tinder (crumpled paper or very dry leaves)
- ☐ Matches or Lighter
- ☐ Adult Supervision

DURATION

DIFFICULTY

WARNING

Fire produces smoke and invisible gases that can be unhealthy for people; make fires only in well-ventilated areas. Keep buckets of water and a hose handy for dousing the fire. Remember: once you start a fire, you are responsible for it until it is completely cold.

Supplementary Data

Why does water put out fire? It's a combination of suffocation (water coats surfaces and prevents air from reaching the flames) and an increase in the energy required for continued combustion (water must be evaporated before the wood can convert to gases suitable for burning).

Cars burn fuel inside a piston and convert the released energy into motion, a process referred to as "internal combustion." Campfires are a form of "external combustion" because they burn fuel in an open pit and the released energy is radiated as heat. Internal combustion systems tend to use the energy in their fuel more efficiently because the released energy is more contained.

Fires produce carbon monoxide – a gas that is both poisonous to humans and a factor in global warming.

HOW-TO

Since no two pieces of wood are identical and wind conditions are always changing, every fire you make will be unique. These instructions should be considered general guidelines and adapted according to your situation as needed.

1. Observe. Determine where the wind, if any, is coming from. Unless there is no wind, a fire has a front and a back. The front is the upwind side, and you will generally want to sit or stand upwind of your fire so that you are not breathing too much smoke.

2. Lay foundation. Select a large piece of wood with a flat face and set it at the back of your fire ring. This will reflect heat and protect the young fire from getting too much wind.

3. Assemble starter. Place a few pieces of tinder at the base of the reflector and lay some kindling against it to form a rough lean-to shape. Place smaller logs on either side of the kindling and leaning up against the reflector.

4. Stockpile. Keep a few medium sized sticks (between kindling and log-sized) at the ready to feed your young fire until the logs ignite. You can use a long thin stick as a poker to move things around in your fire without getting too close to the flames yourself.

5. Ignite. Light the bottom edges of the tinder. Light the bottom so the flames can climb up through the tinder and kindling. Fire likes to go up more than it likes to go down. If the tinder or kindling are damp, you may have to gently blow on the flames to get them to "catch." They may not light at all if they're really wet - try to use dry materials.

6. Feed the fire. As the kindling starts to ignite, carefully lay your medium-sized sticks onto the fire. If you add large pieces too soon, you can crush the young fire before it is strong enough to ignite them.

7. Be efficient. The fire will have a tendency to burn through the middle of the large logs and leave the ends unburned. By nudging the logs closer together as they burn through, you can keep the fire going without adding new logs.

8. Douse. When it's time to put your fire out, be sure to pour water on every surface - even the ash can retain heat and will likely sizzle when watered. After the sizzling stops, stir the ash around to find any dry pockets and pour more water on them. Repeat until everything is cool to the touch.

With some care and feeding, your fire can burn for hours. You can cook potatoes by wrapping them in aluminum foil and placing them at the edges of the fire.

There are other topics in this book that relate to fire, so you may want to take advantage of your fire and do those projects before putting it out.

PROGRESS

Date: ___ / ___ / ___   I did it! ☐

www.fiftydangerousthings.com/topic/45

Super Glue Your Fingers Together

Experience life without a thumb

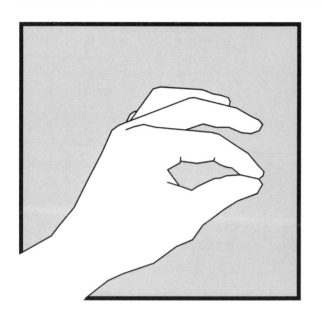

FRUSTRATION

PROPERTY DAMAGE

CUTS AND SCRAPES

REQUIRES

☐ Super Glue
☐ Wax Paper
☐ Nail Polish Remover (optional)

DURATION   **DIFFICULTY**

WARNING

Forcing glued fingers apart can tear the skin; be patient and you will survive unharmed. If you must separate your fingers before the glue releases your fingertips, apply acetone (nail polish remover).

Cover your work area whenever you are using Super Glue. Drops of glue can cause permanent damage to some surfaces and fabrics.

HOW-TO

1. Prepare. Wash your hands and dry completely. Oil and dirt can reduce the effectiveness of the glue.

2. Pick a hand. Decide which hand you are going to experiment on - we recommend using your dominant hand (that's your right hand if you are right-handed).

3. Drip glue. Put a single drop of glue on the pad of your forefinger. With more glue, you run the risk of getting more fingers stuck together.

4. Adhere. Press thumb to forefinger and hold for thirty seconds.

Presto! You have now glued your fingers together. Try doing some normal activities: open a jar of peanut butter, type on a computer, send an SMS on a cell phone, tie your shoes, use a fork.

As your skin exudes moisture and oils and the outer cells naturally slough off, the glue will come unstuck. This may take anywhere from one to four hours.

While your fingers are stuck together, your brain will start to build a new mental map of your hand and its new limitations. This process is performed continually throughout our lives as our bodies grow and age. However, since the mental map of your working thumb and forefinger has been developing since your birth, you will instantly remember how to use your whole hand as soon as your fingers come free.

Supplementary Data

The Original Super Glue and Krazy Glue are brand names for cyanoacrylate adhesives. Cyanoacrylates were invented by scientists at Kodak Laboratories in the early 1940s. They were looking for a glue that could be used to mount gun sights.

With their remarkable ability to stick to skin, cyanoacrylate-based glues are sometimes used instead of sutures to close wounds. Cyanoacrylates are also water resistant and can be used to repair or transplant living corals that have been broken.

There are three basic ways a glue can stick to something. It can either fill up tiny cracks and pores and hold on to those once it hardens, it can have a chemical reaction with the surface, or, like a gecko, it can rely on electrostatic force.

The earliest evidence of glue dates back over 200,000 years.

PROGRESS

Date: ___ / ___ / ___   I did it! ☐

www.fiftydangerousthings.com/topic/46

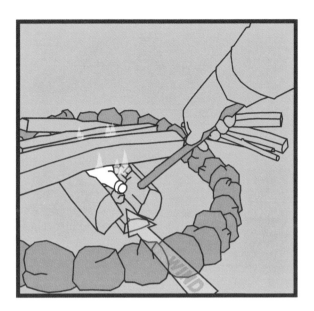

BURNS

SMOKE INHALATION

PROPERTY DAMAGE

REQUIRES

☐ Fire (#45), Water Bucket
☐ Glass Bottle (soda or pill-sized)
☐ Safety Goggles
☐ Adult Supervision

DURATION   **DIFFICULTY**

WARNING

Glass that is heated to the melting point and then cooled quickly can shatter explosively. Make your fire somewhere that you can let it burn itself out rather than dousing it with water.

Supplementary Data

A bellows is designed to draw air into a chamber and then force it out through a small opening pointed at the combustion zone. The extra air makes the fire burn faster and hotter. This is useful for melting glass or metal.

Natural glass is made in volcanoes, by lightning strikes, and meteor impacts. Crude forms of glass can be made by heating sand mixed with the ash created by burning certain kinds of plants. So a fire made on a beach might create a small amount of glass, given the right conditions - which is how many archeologists think that the process was first discovered.

HOW-TO

Firewood typically burns at around 900°F but bottle glass does not melt until almost 1400°F, so we must force the fire to burn hotter by feeding it extra oxygen and constraining the heat to a small area.

1. Prepare your fire area. It must be clear of all combustible material so that you can let your fire burn itself out naturally.

2. Build an oven. Place two large logs side by side with a gap between them only just large enough to lay the bottle in. Align the logs so that the wind blows straight through the gap. This is going to be the combustion zone.

3. Ignition. The upwind side of the gap is the front of your fire, the downwind side will be the exhaust. Place paper and kindling in the front third of the gap and get your fire started.

4. Build up the fire. Once the kindling is really starting to burn, blow gently on it. Feed kindling and larger pieces into the fire until the logs on the either side are burning on their own.

5. Add the bottle. Put on goggles and use a stick to place a bottle at the hottest part of the fire. Place some small firewood across the top of the combustion area to seal in the heat, but make sure the upwind end remains open.

6. Increase the heat. Blow gently and feed medium sized sticks into the combustion area to keep it well fed until the bottle slumps. Slumping happens when the glass becomes so soft that it cannot hold its shape.

7. Cool down. Allow the fire to burn itself out slowly to prevent the glass from shattering due to sudden temperature changes. Once the fire is cool to the touch, use a stick to gently lift the melted bottle from the fire. It may be very fragile, so be careful when handling it.

PROGRESS

Date: ___ / ___ / ___   I did it! ☐

www.fiftydangerousthings.com/topic/47

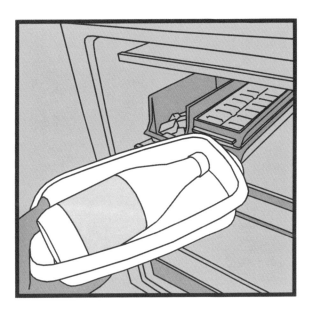

CUTS AND SCRACES

MAKE A MESS

REQUIRES

☐ Sealable Glass Soda Bottle
☐ Plastic Container (to hold the bottle, post explosion)

DURATION   **DIFFICULTY**

WARNING

Broken glass can be incredibly sharp. The slightest touch on an edge can leave you with a nasty cut. Plan how you will dispose of the broken bottle before you put it in the freezer.

Supplementary Data

The expansion of freezing water is the most active process in the dismantling of mountains. Water seeps into tiny cracks in rocks, winter comes, and the water freezes and expands – widening the crack so that more water can get in the next season.

Among all the substances known in modern civilization, water is the only nonmetallic substance that expands in volume as it freezes. As a result, ice floats because it is less dense than liquid water.

Bubbles that you see in ice are formed during the freezing process when dissolved gases are forced out of the water.

An Ice Age is a period when ice covers most of the Earth. Ice ages happen approximately every 40,000 years, but giant meteor impacts, super-volcanoes, and extensive use of carbon-based fuels, can disrupt that cycle.

HOW-TO

This is a great project to do while you are doing something else.

1. Choose your test subject. A glass soda bottle with a screw top will work, and you can drink the soda first and refill it with water for the experiment.

2. Prepare your experiment. Find a plastic container that can hold your bottle and fit into the freezer.

3. Freeze it. Place the container with the bottle in the freezer. You can cover the container with a cloth if you are concerned about bits of glass flying around in your freezer (hint).

4. Wait. Most home refrigerators will take more than an hour to freeze a bottle of water.

5. Check. Gently rock the container to determine if the contents are frozen.

6. Be patient. Repeat steps 4 and 5 until the bottle breaks.

Observe how the bottle broke and try to explain why it broke where it did.

Repeat the experiment with different kinds of bottles. Using a permanent marker, draw on the bottle where you think it will break before you put it in the freezer.

Ice floats. We take this simple fact for granted, but imagine if it weren't so: water would freeze and sink to the cold, dark, bottom of the ocean, never to thaw again. Eventually most of the water in the world would be frozen, except for shallow salty pools near the equator. Brrr.

PROGRESS

Date: ___ / ___ / ___   I did it! ☐

www.fiftydangerousthings.com/topic/48

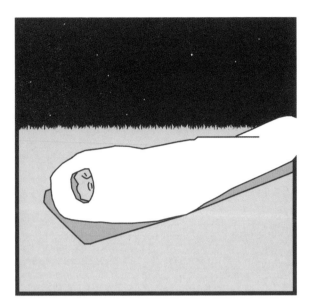

BUGS

COLD

VERMIN

REQUIRES

☐ Sleeping Bag or Blankets
☐ Sleeping Pad (optional)
☐ Pillow (optional)
☐ Flashlight
☐ Tarp

DURATION   **DIFFICULTY**

WARNING

It is rare to find large predators in urban settings, but it does happen occasionally. If that's a concern, check with local animal control services to see if there have been any sightings recently. Clear the path from your sleeping bag back inside - should something happen, you will want a fast route to safety.

HOW-TO

1. Pick your location. Look for an area that is not illuminated by a street or porch light, and clear of any rocks or sticks that might poke you while you are sleeping.

2. Collect your bedding. You will want a sleeping bag or blankets, and a pillow if you want to be luxurious. If it is cold out, you might want a wool cap.

3. Check the weather forecast. If there is humidity, then there may be dew later and you will need a water resistant cover.

4. Assemble your sleeping area. Lay down a tarp, then put your sleeping pad and bedding on top of it.

5. Go to bed. Put your flashlight where you can reach it and climb in for a good night's sleep.

Primitive fight-or-flight instincts are at their most active when we are sleeping in a new place, especially a place where we are not protected by walls. Our hearing becomes more acute as we strain to hear every little noise.

Your imagination becomes very active as you catalog noises and try to figure out what kind of threat is implied. If you let your imagination run wild, you may find yourself scurrying back inside every time a dog barks or the wind shakes the trees.

Supplementary Data

Cowboys of the Old West didn't keep a campfire burning all night just for the warmth. Most animals fear fire and will avoid it even if there is food nearby.

Until recently, it was thought that humans lost 50% of their body heat through their heads. Studies have recently shown that the head loses heat no more quickly than any other exposed part of the body. But when we are bundled up for outdoor activities, the head is often the most exposed part of the body, and so it loses the most heat.

Down feathers are a type of very light fluffy feather that some birds produce. Down is often used in sleeping bags because of its remarkable insulating ability. Down loses its ability to retain heat when it gets wet or is compressed.

Some sleeping bags are rated to -50°F, meaning that a person could sleep outside even if the temperature dropped to 50 degrees below zero.

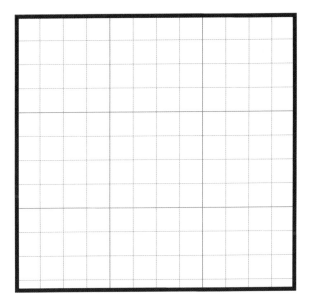

REQUIRES

☐
☐
☐
☐
☐
☐

DURATION   **DIFFICULTY**

WARNING

HOW-TO

1.

2.

3.

4.

5.

6.

Supplementary Data

You might have a grandparent, or a neighbor, who grew up in another country, lived on a farm, or worked in a factory when they were kids. By talking to them about the kinds of things they did for fun when they were kids, you might rediscover an activity that should be in this book.

Field Notes
Observations, improvements, new ideas

Date: ___ / ___ / ___   I did it! ☐

www.fiftydangerousthings.com/topic/50

WHY

Why

Because sometimes you need a good reason

01   Lick a 9-volt Battery

In bypassing the normal sensory processing system and directly activating some of the nerves in our tongue, we are exploring the actual mechanisms of sensing.

02   Play in a Hailstorm

We see so much disaster reported on the news that we often view weather as an unwelcome intrusion in our lives - forgetting that it offers an opportunity to experience the weather, and the world, in a new way.

03   Master the Perfect Somersault

Somersaults are not dangerous.

04   Kiss Hello Like the French

By learning a new kind of greeting, we develop a greater appreciation of the subtle aspects of other cultures and a deeper understanding of our own sense of personal space and sources of embarrassment.

05   Stick Your Hand out the Window

Anyone can develop an intuitive understanding of the effects of lift and drag - key concepts in aerodynamics - by flying their hand like a wing. The open window is a wind tunnel accessible to everyone.

06   Drive a Nail

Pounding a nail into a board sounds trivial, but it actually requires finesse. Our world is held together with nails, and learning what it takes to really drive a nail gives us an appreciation for the people who do it and highlights the difference between knowing what something is and knowing how to do it.

07   Drive a Car

Children spend so much time being driven around in cars that they take the process for granted. Cartoons show steering as spinning the wheel back and forth like a crazy person; actually piloting a car recalibrates a child's mental model and helps them understand that the adult who is driving is actually busy. It is an empowering moment when a child takes control of a massive machine.

Why

Because sometimes you need a good reason

08 Throw a Spear

Our brains are uniquely wired for throwing things. In throwing spears we perform internal calculus, predict the outcome, process visual feedback, and integrate the results. Every throw is like a scientific experiment.

09 Make a Bomb in a Bag

We are composed of chemical compounds, surrounded by chemical compounds, and consuming chemical compounds, but we don't often have the chance to play with chemistry just for the sake of exploration. A simple chemical reaction that we can experiment with provides the conceptual foundation for a deeper understanding of the elemental and chemical nature of our universe.

10 Play with the Vacuum Cleaner

When moving air is constrained to small tubes or spaces it begins to exhibit some peculiar properties (such as vortices, venturi, shock waves). Since air currents are typically difficult to see, being able to interact and play with them provides a valuable opportunity to make sense of these phenomena.

11 Throw Rocks

The moment that you pick up a rock, you become responsible for what happens to it. Learning to throw a rock improves our ability to throw anything. Even structure of our shoulders has developed to support this specific motion.

12 Play with Dry Ice

Carbon dioxide is a compound with an unusual property: sublimation. Whenever scientific properties can be visualized and explored directly, it provides an opportunity to understand more intuitively, rather than simply learn. When dry ice vaporizes water it makes the gas visible, creating a new array of scientific explorations.

13 Boil Water in a Paper Cup

We don't usually think of water that is boiling as being cool, but by contrasting it to things that are much hotter we can see that cool is a relative term. The physics of combustion is commonly understood as fire igniting paper and being suppressed by water; this familiar relationship is simply presented in an unexpected setting.

14 Put Strange Stuff in the Microwave

We take kitchen appliances - and the other devices we interact with every day - for granted; by the time we turn five we hardly give them a second thought. The magnetron in a microwave oven is as powerful a tool for scientific inquiry as a microscope.

Why
Because sometimes you need a good reason

15 **Throw Things from a Moving Car**

Wind resistance is a form of drag; however, it's not until we exaggerate the effect that one develops a real sense of it. Everything that moves or is thrown is effected by drag; multiply the effect and it becomes immediately tangible. "Thin air" isn't so thin after all.

16 **Drop from High Places**

Practicing how to fall helps us learn to treat impact with the ground sensibly, and knowing how to fall safely can defuse some irrational panic that otherwise can make falling more dangerous. Some activities are dangerous only because of the risk of injury in the event of a fall - the spectre of danger is disarmed with the ability to land without harm.

17 **Burn Things with a Magnifying Glass**

Refraction is less intuitive than reflection; playing with a lens helps us integrate the concept. Sunlight delivers a huge amount of energy to the surface of the planet - using a lens to concentrate it makes that energy tangible, in a potentially surprising way.

18 **Walk Home from School**

Walking stimulates the brain and reduces anxiety. The habit of walking pays dividends over a lifetime: improved memory, consistent exercise, independence, and a sense of well-being. Despite the headlines to the contrary, children are safer walking than being driven the same distance.

19 **Stand on the Roof**

The peak of the roof is a child-sized Mount Everest; getting safely up and down from the peak is no less an accomplishment than Reinhold Messner's first ascent.

20 **Squash Pennies on a Railroad Track**

While we must respect the danger of being near a moving train, it's important to learn not to panic - getting scared and running away might put us in more danger. A squashed penny is a powerful demonstration of the weight and force of a train.

21 **Spend an Hour Blindfolded**

Experience life without sight. We take our senses for granted, and you never know how much you need something until it is gone. Loss of sight gives us an appreciation of the complexity and surprising richness of everyday life for the blind.

Why
Because sometimes you need a good reason

22
Bend Steel
Inside the "black box" of a computer is a complex arrangement of electronics and programming - which can be understood and ultimately manipulated. Raw materials are their own sort of "black box"; recognizing that they can also be understood and manipulated is not just intellectually satisfying but can also be creatively empowering.

23
Break Glass
We are trained never to break anything, especially glass. This can lead to feelings of fear and panic when it happens accidentally, neither of which are useful when dealing with broken glass. Doing it deliberately a few times defuses the built-up anxiety and trepidation.

24
Construct Your Own Flying Machine
Dry cleaner bag hot air balloons are a visual illustration of just how much lighter hot air is than cold air. Using a hot air dryer for a project like this helps us see our home appliances as tools and scientific instruments, rather than strictly single purpose mechanisms.

25
Look at the Sun
Constructing an apparatus for viewing the sun shows that we can answer a question - what does the surface of the sun look like? - for ourselves, and that we can all participate in scientific inquiry.

26
Learn Dramatic Sword Fighting
The sword fighting that we see in movies is the result of a carefully choreographed sequence of moves. Like learning a magician's trick, knowing how to fake a sword fight is a way to understand what we see when we watch movies. The illusion relies on the cooperation of the participants, morphing the activity from implied conflict to close collaboration.

27
Make a Slingshot
A slingshot is really just another tool; using one expands the mental model of our body. Slingshots are also an invitation to mischief; we learn self-control by exploring the limits of acceptable behavior and demonstrating that we can be trusted.

28
Climb a Tree
Climbing a tree is a great opportunity to spend some time really looking at how trees grow and heal themselves, and to notice the amazing structures that have evolved to handle the weight of the branches and the forces of wind. There is a unique feeling of freedom that comes from being up in a tree, above your parents, and away from the cares of the world.

Why
Because sometimes you need a good reason

29 Perform on the Street

Overcoming our initial embarrassment and actually offering something to a crowd of strangers develops self-confidence. It is not only great practice for public speaking, but a valuable foundation for all future interpersonal interactions: interviews, negotiations, conflict resolution, to name but a few.

30 Dam up a Creek

Playing with water, and understanding how water pressure and erosion work, is hands-on learning, and the creek is a perfect context for self-directed physics, engineering, and biology experiments. Making dams is great way to have a discussion about the individual and collective impact of our actions on the ecosystem.

31 Go Underground

Going underground, underwater, or into space, is a serious undertaking and should not be done lightly. These hostile environments operate on different rules and our natural instincts may be completely inappropriate. A culvert or storm drain is a good way to experience, and develop a respect for, the differences first hand.

32 Change a Tire

The confidence to self-rescue is built by exercising our ability to perform critical tasks. Changing a tire before being able to drive changes the mental model of the car from impenetrable conveyance to manufactured device capable of being fixed. Reading the owners manual is a great exercise in understanding and interpreting written directions.

33 Dive in a Dumpster

What one person thinks of as garbage, another person may find immensely valuable. A dumpster with interesting stuff in it is a perfect example of this and it helps us think about the potential value of what we throw out.

34 Deconstruct an Appliance

We treat the appliances in our daily lives like magic boxes, never considering the bits and pieces that they are made from. Every manufactured object can be broken down into ever simpler parts until there is nothing left that we can't understand. Once disassembled, often there are parts that can be reused or repurposed that might otherwise have been discarded.

35 Go to the Dump

Seeing, first hand, what happens to our garbage makes us more conscious of the ecological impact of our habits.

36 ### Poison Your Friends

Choosing who among your friends to trick forces us to think about what friendship is and what it means. Dealing with the aftermath of the breach of trust may require sincerity, thoughtfulness, and patience.

37 ### Fly Your Homemade Kite in a Gale

Kites are a form of simple wing and minor adjustments can make major improvements in the flight behavior. Seeing firsthand how small changes create big changes builds important intuition skills. Spending time outside in stormy weather is exhilarating, and flying a kite in bad weather reinforces the idea that weather can be interesting, not simply an inconvenience.

38 ### Learn Tightrope Walking

Feeling confident on unfamiliar footing is always a benefit, whether you're working on a roof, crossing a creek using a log, or making a presentation to a room full of strangers. Separating the fear of failure (falling) from the essential skill (walking) is a lesson that can be applied in a multitude of circumstances as well.

39 ### Cook Something in the Dishwasher

There are many sources of heat in our daily lives; taking advantage of that waste energy and using it to get useful work done is a form of conservation. Exploring how else our most common household items can be used helps us start to see the potential inherent in all devices.

40 ### Find a Beehive

Social insects represent a unique class of evolved behaviors; spending time watching and thinking about them is an accessible form of biological investigation. Bees are a critical component of the human biosphere, responsible for pollinating more than two-thirds of the plants we rely on. Of all the projects in this book, this might be impossible to complete: failure is always an option.

41 ### Cross Town on Public Transit

Our world gets bigger with every journey we take. Public transit is one of the safest ways to get around a city, and learning to use it is empowering.

42 ### Break the Recipe Rule Book

Baking is a science that tolerates a lot of mistakes. Making up your own recipe is a great way to get comfortable in the kitchen. A spectacular disaster or serendipitous success will only encourage more experiments.

Why
Because sometimes you need a good reason

43 **Whittle**

Activities where we repeat a motion and watch the results develop our tool-using skills. The more we practice holding and using a single tool, the more we are able to pick up and use other tools as well. The pocketknife is typically the first multi-purpose tool we get our hands on, and owning one changes how we see the world and empowers us to be agents of change.

44 **Make a Rope Swing**

A swing is a simple contraption that gives hours of engaged play. Time spent on a swing is an opportunity to understand our vestibular system, embrace the concept of gravity as a form of acceleration, and to cogitate.

45 **Play with Fire**

The open fire is a laboratory and an invitation to explore the properties of one of the most elemental forces in nature - it is hands-on science of the most engaging sort. As with other dangerous activities, becoming familiar with the risks and responsibilities of building a fire ultimately reduces the liklihood of a truly dangerous result.

46 **Super Glue Your Fingers Together**

A temporary disability can help us to better appreciate our usual physical condition. Necessity is the mother of invention; having to figure out how to accomplish our everyday tasks in spite of glued fingers forces us to be creative. If taken far enough, the new kinesthetic map created while fingers are glued will be strong enough to cause unfamiliarity when the fingers are unglued.

47 **Melt Glass**

Making a fire is relatively easy; making a fire that can do serious work is more complicated but is fully understandable. Seeing that an ordinary campfire can be coaxed into producing enough heat to melt glass shows that we can never make assumptions about fire.

48 **Explode a Bottle in the Freezer**

Common processes at work in nature exert incredible, inexorable, forces on the things we make.

49 **Sleep in the Wild**

We forget that it was once common to sleep outside. The familiar area around our home becomes a whole new world after dark, and we see - and hear - things in a whole new way.

Why

Because sometimes you need a good reason

Your Project

Exploring the dangerous margins of creativity is as essential as the safe, frequented center.

Author's Notes

Favorite Web Resources and Vendors

Wikipedia, the online encyclopedia: en.wikipedia.org
Make Magazine, technology on your time: makezine.com
Exploratorium, the world's greatest science museum: exploratorium.org
Free-Range Kids, dedicated to sane parenting: freerangekids.com
Solarbotics, electronics kits and parts: solarbotics.com
TechShop, open-access, public workshops: techshop.ws
Instructables, how-to and DIY projects: instructables.com
TED, inspiring ideas: ted.com
Pop!Tech, more inspiring ideas: poptech.com
Google Docs, online editing and collaboration tools: docs.google.com
Adobe Systems, makers of fine book development tools: adobe.com
CreateSpace, print-on-demand self-publishing and distribution: createspace.com
Tinkering School, where it all started: tinkeringschool.com
Fifty Dangerous Things, and more: fiftydangerousthings.com

How This Book Was Made

It all started with a mention in a presentation at TED 2007: Five Dangerous Things You Should Let Your Children Do (http://on.ted.com/272G). The presentation was posted online where more than two million people have watched it, many of whom started asking about the book. After trying several different approaches to get it published by tradition-al means, we decided to do it ourselves.

We began by collecting potential topic ideas in a Google Spreadsheet. Each topic was marked with a list of possible dangers, expected duration, difficulty, and so forth. That list grew to more than 80 possible topics; from there we sifted and sorted until we had the best 50. While the list was being refined, versions of possible page designs (inspired by af-ter-market car repair books) were generated and reviewed with friends and designers. That said, all of the poor design choices herein are the fault of our own inabilities to execute on the excellent advice and design feedback we received. Each topic was expanded into a separate Google Document and versions were sent to volunteers to review and test.

Meanwhile, illustrations were created in Adobe Illustrator. Because the topic categories (Activity, Project, Experience, and Skill) had yet to be finalized, every illustration had to be created in a way that let us pick the base color at the last moment. As feedback came in, the topics were refined and updated. The final layout was still not quite ready, so these versions of the topics were ported to XML so that they could be ingested by Adobe InDesign. The page was set up so content would automatically flow into whatever became the final design (made more interesting by the fact that this was the first time Julie had ever used InDesign). Perforce was used to version-track all of the XML and InDesign files and scripts (and should have been used for the illustrations as well).

While Gever was at a conference in Qatar, Julie threw together a cover design in Adobe Photoshop and an alpha test print of the book was produced to check colors and margins. Little did we know, her Photoshop project would take on a life of its own and be the on-going hiccup in our otherwise orderly Illustrator/XML/InDesign-based workflow. Third-draft versions of the topics were updated in XML to fit into the latest, and near-final, version of the page layout. These were sent to a smaller group of dedicated testers. Colors for the topics were chosen and two copies of a beta-version of the book were printed. During this review (which included extensive fact-checking), hazard icons were created, the book front and back cover designs were refined, and the front-matter (foreword, introduction, table of contents, etc.) was finalized as well. Final feedback was integrated and the last tweaks were made in InDesign. This page was written, and then the book was rendered as a PDF and sent to the CreateSpace print-on-demand facility.

Total elapsed time: three months of continuous effort while laundry and email piled up.

Because of the process and the tools we are using, this book can easily be rendered to different page sizes and differ-ent output media. Every bit of this book was made by Julie and Gever, but we couldn't have done it without all the help from family and friends. Your suggestions and feedback will help us improve future efforts: gever@fiftydangerousthings.com

gever & julie, december 2009

7573422R0

Made in the USA
Lexington, KY
01 December 2010